HORSE CRAZY!

Dog Town Press
2007

www.horsecrazy.net

Horse Crazy!

A Tongue-in-Cheek Guide for Parents of Horse-Addicted Girls

Bob Goddard

To Sincerely Yours, Bruiser, Guy, Jay, Aslan, Quando, Jazz, Image, Eddie, Waders, Chilli, Bert and the other nine million domesticated horses in North America. How bored we would be without you.

Table of Contents

CHAPTER 1:

The Second Most Powerful Force in the Universe

I should have seen it coming. I'm a good parent and I should have seen it coming. The warning signs were clear enough.

The first thing I noticed was the hat. Why was Jamie wearing that hat? And who gave her those boots?

It's just a phase, I told myself.

Then came the mood swings. Dark and sullen one moment, cheerleader-happy the next. But even when she was euphoric, communication was difficult. Her speech was laced with a jargon that made it sound like a foreign language. "Snaffle bit!" she once blurted out at the dinner table.

Who was this girl?

A new circle of friends appeared. Phone conversations whispered in conspiratorial tones became a nightly ritual. These kids were up to something. Something sinister. Something treacherous. Something expensive. And they were drawing Jamie deeper and deeper into their world.

She will grow out of this, I prayed.

But then, during a teary-eyed confession on a sleepless August night, Jamie admitted to me her loyalty to the Indianapolis Colts. And that's when the awful truth hit home: the girl was completely and hopelessly horse crazy. And before I could absorb the news, another shock: "Hiliary secretly roots for the Denver Broncos, Dad."

Horse crazy! How could this happen? Why couldn't they get into drugs or gangs like normal kids? Why horses? Why me?

This was a crisis. Something had to be done, and soon. But what? Like any sensible husband, I turned to my wife:

"This is your fault, Jenny."

"Bob, it's not anybody's 'fault'. The girls are developing new interests - that's all."

"You don't understand. They're horse crazy! Do you know what that means?"

"Of course I do, honey. They're horse *crazy*. It means they're definitely your children. You need to relax."

"Relax? Listen, we're the parents and we should be in control around here."

"We *are* in control. At least one of us is."

"You're the one who gave Jamie that horse sticker book."

"What horse sticker book?"

"When she was seven. You bought it for her."

"That was six years ago!" protested Jenny.

"And Hiliary's rocking horse. That was your idea too."

"She was three years old..."

"Why did you encourage them?"

"You're making way too big a deal about this, Bob. It's not like we're going to turn our lives upside down because the girls talk about horses."

"It's a crisis!"

"Nobody said we're actually going to get a horse right now. We'll just take it one step at a time."

That was thirteen years ago. Since then, we've been through nine horses, attended one hundred eighty-two horse shows, bought three horse trailers, ruined two trucks, moved to the country, built a barn, spent all our money, and then spent some more. We bought every kind of saddle ever made. We assembled a remarkable collection of tack and over priced show outfits. We wrote countless checks for vets and farriers and horse dentists. We used up seven different trainers. Our weekends, our summers, and the girls' inheritance disappeared into a black hole of equine mania.

Of course, I didn't actually know all this was going to happen. I just had a sense that we were dealing with something that went beyond the normal "I Want a Pony" thing. This was far more serious. And it wasn't just about money. This thing could actually threaten our way of life. Would I still have time to feed my addiction to computer games? How many reruns of *Star Trek* would I miss? Was pro football in jeopardy?

Jenny's response was a mystery. The woman is an intelligent, practical person – an *accountant* for Pete's sake. In all other matters she was our voice of reason and good sense. She was the one who persuaded me not to quit my job as a caregiver at a veterans' home when I wanted to run for president in 1988. She was the one who talked Jamie out of applying to the Air Force Academy at age 11. And she is the one who kept Hiliary from roller-blading off the roof of our house in order to impress the neighbor boy or his dog, I wasn't sure which. But when it came to horses, Jenny became a misty-eyed enabler. And she was not pulling any punches. A week after Jamie's late night confession, she hit me with "Bob, we need to talk."

We need to talk. Normally Jenny would use this phrase to initiate a conversation that would culminate in my offering an apology for something. It could be for something I did, but didn't know, or it could be for something I didn't do and still didn't know. I cut through the preliminaries:

"Jenny, I'm sorry and I promise to do better next time."

"No, we need to talk about Hiliary and Jamie. I'm thinking a horse might not be such a bad idea."

This was getting out of hand.

"Are you sure you wouldn't rather talk about something I did or didn't do?"

"It would be nice if they had something they could do together."

"Couldn't we just buy them a tandem bike? And what happened to one step at time? We're not ready for this. We don't have the money, we don't have the stuff, and we don't know what we're doing."

"That didn't stop us from getting married, did it Bob?"

A "nag" analogy popped into my head, but I held my tongue.

"Look Bob, we don't have to jump in all at once. The girls met some people in 4-H who are willing to lease a horse to us. We can keep him at their barn and all we have to do is pay for the upkeep. We can go from there."

They met some "people" in 4-H? What was she thinking? Clearly, she did not comprehend the true nature of this organization. People think 4-H is such a wonderful thing, but it's no place for a horse crazy kid. Sending a horse-crazed kid to 4-H is like holding AA meetings at the neighborhood pub. People in 4-H LOVE horses. 4-H is an evil cult of true believers and a source of the most radical, pro-horse-ownership propaganda imaginable. Kids come home from 4-H meetings not only believing that owning a horse is possible, but that it's wholesome fun and builds character. Like I said, 4-H is evil.

(Author's Disclaimer: throughout this guide you will find several references to 4-H. As most of you know, 4-H stands for "Hogs, Horses, Heifers, and Hounds." Actually,

4

4-H is a great organization. It provides kids with a great way to become involved with horses – or a variety of other animals for that matter. It's mainly about learning and responsibility. I highly recommend this organization. My only objection to 4-H is its vicious plan to take over the world and enslave humanity.)

It was only through sheer trickery that the girls got into 4-H in the first place. It started when Jamie approached me about joining an organization called Sunset Riders. Like any other self-distracted father, I said "Well, sure!"

Allow me to describe the level of my naivety at that moment. I assumed Sunset Riders was some kind of horse appreciation group where people sat around, ate cookies, and talked about how much they loved horses and how great it would be to actually have one. As we all know, no such group has ever existed anywhere in the United States of America. This was a *riding* group. And they used *real* horses. The name Sunset *Riders* should have tipped me off.

Of course, Jamie neglected to mention that Sunset Riders was a 4-H club. And she didn't bother to tell me that every last kid in that 4-H club had a horse. And she forgot to point out that the club put on monthly horse shows. I even drove Hiliary and Jamie to their first meeting, unaware of the trap that had been set. This pattern of deceit and manipulation was to be repeated many times in the next thirteen years.

So here was our dilemma. Unless we were going to allow our girls to bounce around a show ring horseless, like characters in *Monty Python and the Holy Grail*, we had to do something. But did Jenny seriously think these two could share a horse? Obviously, she hadn't looked in their bedrooms lately.

Mathematically, Jamie (14) and Hiliary (9) were five years apart. But in terms of personality and temperament, they were from different planets. Their bedrooms were monuments to their differences.

In Jamie's room, the bed was always made, complete with hospital corners. I often wondered if she actually slept under the covers. Two large bookcases supported a book collection that was sorted and labeled according to the Dewey Decimal System. Four long cardboard boxes, each containing bedroom decorations for a season were stacked under her bed. The walls were adorned with a *Top Gun* poster, a picture of Gandhi, and the American flag. Her stuffed animals were arranged in a perfect pyramid on a 32-inch shelf above her bed, exactly midway between the walls. A badly worn but intact Mickey Mouse doll, which her grandmother had given her when she was 3 months old, perched at the top of the pyramid, surveying it all.

I was never quite sure if Hiliary even had a bed. There was a place where the layer of tangled clothes – clean, dirty, undefined – and miscellaneous items rose higher off the floor, and I assumed that was her bed, but no one ever really knew. An autographed photo of Jim Carey was taped to the wall above her dresser, just over her copy of *Mystery Science Theater 3000, the Movie*, which was missing the case. A poster of John Lennon looked down on us from the ceiling. Breyer horse models peeked out from every nook and cranny. Pictures of Hiliary Herself could be found if you dug around the room long enough. As often as not, these featured something inappropriate, like a kitchen doily or a cat on her head. If she was angry at one of us, we would find one of *our* pictures on the floor - outside her bedroom door.

The idea that these polar opposites could work together on anything without creating a mass disturbance in the balance of the universe - or at least the psycho/emotional balance of our family - had to be one of the most optimistic notions of the 20th Century. However, the girls did have one significant thing in common; they both took great pride and pleasure in their ability to manipulate and deceive their father. When infused with the power of horse craziness, the Improbable Alliance of Sisters with\the support of their hopelessly insane mother proved too strong for me to resist. They got their damn horse.

What I've learned from our horse-centered life is the subject of this book. I wish to share with you, the parents of horse-crazed girls, my vast knowledge of these curiously headstrong creatures. I will discuss things like what to feed them, how to keep them under control, and how to keep yourself safe around them. I have a great deal to say about horses as well.

What About You?

If you are new to horsegirl parenting, you are probably feeling a little confused. Perhaps you even feel overwhelmed. Be assured that millions of parents have gone through what you are now experiencing. And most of them would agree with the following advice. Hide. Run away and hide. Do it now. Put down this book and make yourself invisible. Find an empty closet or some attic space, or go to your sister's in St. Louis. Defect to Mexico. It's cheaper and it may be your last chance to maintain any trace of sanity.

Of course, I realize you aren't going anywhere. A part of you hopes you can continue living a normal life, despite the fact that your daughter is deeply disturbed. *Oh, a horse is no big deal,* you tell yourself. Or perhaps you're still in denial. You think all this is temporary and that it's natural for a girl her age to want a horse. You're sure she'll forget about horses when she discovers boys.

I have news for you. A tidal wave is coming, and you are in its path. If your kid has a genuine case of horse craziness, she will not "just forget about it." She will plead. She will promise. She will plot. *She will tell Grandma.* And she will never, ever give up. That eighty pounds of sheer determination standing in front of you is a product of the Second Most Powerful Force in the Universe. No earthly power can hold out forever against a young girl's desire to have a horse of her own. You will delay. You will compromise. You will distract. You will say NO a thousand times. You will lose.

I suppose you could forget about this book and educate yourself with a serious guide for parents of horse-crazed kids. There are many available. But why bother? Some parents have been doing this for years and *still* don't have a clue. And they're doing just fine (sort of). As long as you have no real choice about any of this, you might as well relax and have some FUN. So, whether you're a new horse parent or you've been having FUN for years, this book is for you.

This book is also for anyone who has ever been horse crazy. You need to know how much trouble you've caused.

CHAPTER 2:

The Horsepeople Culture

Horse craziness is a disease that affects the mind. But don't tell a horseperson that. Most horsepeople reject the notion that their passion for horses is a mental illness. Some are offended by the idea. But I don't mean it that way. The victims of horse disease aren't insane - they just drive everyone around them nuts.

Horse disease typically strikes between the ages of eight and thirteen. The victims are overwhelmingly female. Why girls? What is it about the female psyche that draws them to horses? While nobody knows for sure, there are theories. Freud, for instance, had something to say about the horse disease. Dr. Freud believed females are subconsciously envious of the male's ability to pee when they're standing up. From this, he quite reasonably concluded that girls have an unconscious desire to do away with their mothers. The insurance money and survivor's benefits could then be used to purchase a horse. I know it sounds a bit contorted, but that's Freud for you.

Others compare the nurturing instinct of the female with the male's primary instinct to break things. The "Non-Specific Theory of Gender Roles Concerning Big Animal Loving" contends that because of some kind of genetic something-or-other, the female has more of some kind of peculiar chambers or chemicals in her brain than the male. This somehow makes her better suited to take care of large animals or whatever. On the other hand, a male's basic mental design makes him more interested in tearing apart that Western saddle than he is in putting it on a horse. This same design also makes him intensely interested in leaving the pieces scattered all over the floor.

The Course of the Disease

The typical horsegirl goes through several phases prior to full-blown horse disease. The first is the *Infant Phase*. At this stage, the girl doesn't say much about it. This is because she is an infant and hasn't learned how to talk. These are relatively peaceful years for the parent.

By the time the child is able to walk – she won't. She will want to ride everywhere and on everything. Anything that moves will be a target: her big wheel, her brother's wagon, the vacuum cleaner, Dad's shoulders, Uncle Jim's foot. The cat.

Some parents believe that a child's fascination with penny-a-ride supermarket horses and merry-go-rounds is an early indication of horse disease. This is a fallacy. These activities are far too inexpensive to be considered remotely related to horse disease. On the other hand, if the kid demanded that you buy the penny-a-ride supermarket horse and haul it home in the back of the minivan, then it would be a genuine sign of horse disease.

The *Infant Phase* is followed by the *Learning Phase*. This is when you send your child to school to learn. The first thing she learns is that there is a girl in her school WHO ALREADY HAS A HORSE. Your girl will hate this girl. She will hate her with a bloody passion that defies description. But instead of being mean to Already-Has-A-Horse Girl, your daughter will suck up to her. She'll do anything she can to ride that horse.

Your daughter's association with Little Miss Suzy Hasahorse introduces her to the tangible reality of horse ownership. Before this, owning a horse was merely a distant dream, a faraway fantasy. But once she witnesses the phenomenon first hand, the parental idea of nipping it in the bud becomes the fantasy. Now that she has seen it with her own eyes, there is no going back; the genie has been released from the bottle, the apple has been eaten, the Rubicon has been crossed, and the snowball is in Hell.

By the time the girl is ten or eleven, the disease becomes fully active. This is known as the *Military Phase*. Now she is prepared to launch a brutal campaign of emotional and psychological terror upon her parents. Military historians would classify this level of conflict as "total war." A no-holds-barred contest. She will bombard you with unending requests for horse magazines, videos, and trips to the local riding stable. She will form get-the-poor-kid-a-horse alliances with friends and relatives who have no financial stake in the matter. She will blitz your defenses with pouts and tears and lethal looks. She will wear down your resistance by holding fake horse shows in the front yard using brooms and empty milk bottles. She will give her bike a name.

After a few months of this, parents of horse-diseased daughters will find themselves rummaging through the house for any type of white material. They need it for the flag. It takes a little time, but most parents eventually come to the conclusion that surrendering is the only way to peace. The surrender ceremony consists of the parent signing the Document of Capitulation (a check to a horse seller) while the victorious girl observes from her vantage point atop her brand new horse. "I need a better saddle," she announces.

With her new horse, the girl becomes an active participant in the horsepeople culture. Prepare yourself: she is going to develop some new personality traits. These traits are common to this subculture and they will be with her for the rest of her life. Coping with all of this requires patience, understanding, love, and a revolving credit account.

In order to understand the horsepeople culture, you must accept one simple truth: *horsepeople are not like the rest of us*. They may look like we do. They may occasionally talk like we do. They may even attempt to act like we do. But sooner or later, it will become abundantly clear that they are *nothing* like us. And they like it that way.

Once you accept the fact that horsepeople are inherently different, things will start to make sense. You will begin to understand that your horsegirl's bizarre behavior patterns and oddball habits are merely the accepted norms and practices of a distinct sub-culture. In other words, they're *all* a bit peculiar.

Living with a horsegirl (or horsewoman), (or horseboy), (or horseman), (or horseundecided) puts you in direct contact with this alien culture. Living next to them isn't all that easy either. This has nothing to do with race or religion or ethnic background or sexual preference (some like mares, some like geldings, and others prefer stallions). Also, horsepeople culture cuts across all socioeconomic classes. Be aware that while horse ownership is a traditional mark of wealth and status, it's also really good at creating poverty.

Beliefs and Traits of the Horsepeople Culture

What makes horsepeople unique are their priorities and how they express those priorities in everyday behavior. This can be seen in their beliefs, traits, and attitudes. Be warned: some of these are frightening to outsiders. The following list is the result of minutes and minutes of research and hours and hours of thinking about what I found out.

Equine Transference Complex. This trait manifests itself in every waking moment of a horsegirl's day. From the time she rises to the time she goes to bed, she makes a constant effort to turn everything she sees, hears, or feels into a horse-related experience. While she is away from her daily horsey routine, she is like a dolphin out of water, desperately and sometimes pathetically searching for the "horse side" of any experience. She roots for the Indianapolis Colts even though she hates football. In a department store, you will find her at the magazine rack, perusing the horse publications, even though she has every single one of them at home. While riding in the car, she comments on every horse farm, horse trailer, and hay field. While channel surfing, she is unable to switch past any channel displaying horses, even if it is a bad western. At the video store, she studies the jacket covers of *Black Beauty* and *The Horse Whisperer* even though she's seen these thirty-seven times each. Certain beer commercials and cigarette ads mesmerize her, even though she thinks these products are disgusting.

Equine Idiomatic Generalization. This is the inadvertent use of horsey words and phrases in non-horsey situations. Examples include such things as saying "whoa" to the dog or "giddyup" to the car. A wife may instruct her husband that it's past time to "muck the garage" and a daughter may tell her father that he needs to be "groomed" before leaving the house. A shopper in the back of the line at Wal-Mart may make clicking sounds in an attempt to get the checkout lane moving faster.

The Tarzan Syndrome. This is in reference to a horsegirl's underlying desire to live among The Horses, the same way Tarzan lived with The Apes. It begins as a mild annoyance with any activity that requires time away from her horse. Things like schoolwork, household chores, a job, or a boyfriend are regarded as a waste of precious horse time. As the desire grows in intensity, she may also begin to neglect such basic activities as supper, going to the bathroom, and sleep. Thus, it is not unusual to find a horsegirl taking her meals in the barn, peeing in the stalls, and threatening to sleep in the hayloft. During nice weather, she may disappear from the house for days or even weeks. (You are still allowed to claim her as a dependent at tax time).

Equine Metamorphic Ideation. The horsegirl is not content to merely be with the horses; she wants to *become* a horse. Do not confuse this with natural riding techniques that encourage the rider to mentally "become one" with the horse. This is more extreme. She yearns to undergo some kind of bizarre metamorphosis and become a horse, like Jeff Goldblum became The Fly or like George W. became President of the United States. At first, she merely identifies with the horses; she follows their moods, watches their behavior, and mimics their actions. But this only intensifies her curiosity. She craves to know what it would feel like to gallop around in that massive body, to fully comprehend the nickers and neighs of her stable mates, and to feel the satisfaction of eating grass and hay without barfing. She's not crazy; she knows none of this is possible. But that doesn't lessen her desire. She dreams about it at night.

Horsey Fashion. What kind of clothes do horsepeople wear? A stereotype puts them in t-shirts, jeans, boots, and a cowboy hat. While horsepeople wear these things sometimes, it does not make them unique. Anybody can wear that stuff. What really sets them apart is the phenomenon of Barn Clothes. The idea behind Barn Clothes is simple: every article of clothing a horseperson owns is designated as either Barn Clothes (to be worn exclusively for barn work or work with the horses) or Future Barn Clothes. Yeah, they have nice stuff, but it's only a matter of time before it becomes baptized with hay, sawdust, manure, mud, fly spray, or horsehair. This often happens when the horseperson is in a hurry and doesn't have time to put on proper barn clothes before performing some aspect of horse care, e.g., throwing a flake of hay to the horses before work or school. At the moment the virgin clothes are initiated, the horseperson utters a perfunctory, "Oh, darn, I ruined my good (shoes) (slacks) (blouse) (socks) (pajamas)," then happily adds it to her inventory of Barn Clothes.

Standards of Cleanliness. Are horsepeople dirty? The horseperson's typical indifference to house dirt is not a sign she is unclean. Instead, experts believe that this is a result of a subconscious desire to bring the barn into the house. The horseperson is simply making a symbolic attempt to be closer to what she holds dear. The small

15

amount of dirt in specific areas of the house is merely a token of this desire, and thus harmless. Do not hold it against her.

Social Life. Contrary to popular opinion, horsepeople are capable of having social contact outside their circle of horsepeople friends. They just don't think it's necessary. They recognize the existence of Those Outside the Body and are able to tolerate the company of The Others – for a few minutes, anyway.

Extended periods away from Those Like Her can lead to unfortunate consequences. For example, if a horseperson finds herself sitting at restaurant table with a large group of non-horsepeople whose primary topics of conversation consist of the weather, gardening, and Hilary Clinton, she may, without warning, simply explode. The eruption often comes in the form of a verbal spewing of unrelated horse terms, "Equitation, gallop, lead rope! Reins, sidesaddle, Pinto! Hocks! Withers! Green broke! Green broke! Green broke!" For bystanders who are unacquainted with the horsepeople culture, this can be disturbing. But it's no big deal to those of us who have been around it for years. "We've seen worse," we like to say.

Astonishing Patience (In Certain Situations). In certain situations, horsepeople are capable of exercising a remarkable degree of patience. This is often seen at horse shows. For example, most horse shows start with showmanship classes. Since the judge must personally inspect each and every horse and handler, these classes can take a long time to complete. To an outsider, a typical horseshow schedule seems like this:

8 a.m. Showmanship
9 a.m. Showmanship
10 a.m. Showmanship
11 a.m. Showmanship

Noon Showmanship
1 p.m. Showmanship
2 p.m. Showmanship
Year 2023 Showmanship
Until Hell freezes over: Showmanship
 I don't know how they can stand it. While the rest of us have shifted in our seats a hundred fifteen times, made seven trips to the restroom, strolled around the show grounds five times, laid down, gotten up, sat in the truck, sat on the truck, sat under the truck, the real horsepeople camp around the show ring for hours on end, completely absorbed in what is going on in the ring. And they do this *every* weekend.

 Attitudes Toward Danger. In most cases, horsepeople view danger the same as anybody else. They have a healthy respect for hazardous situations and places: railroad crossings, busy interstates, rattlesnakes, narrow mountain roads, high school cafeterias, auditioning for *American Idol.* However, when it comes to horses, they're stupid. A horse that bolts into the woods with a rider aboard is "just having fun." A pair of horses attempting to kick the crap out of each other while you happen to be in between them is nothing to worry about, because "they're just playing." Trotting the horse past a noisy construction site is a great way to "prepare him for showing."

 Belief in the Superiority of One's Own Horse. Horsepeople talk about their horses the same way grandparents talk about their grandchildren. They believe, quite literally, that their poop does not stink. Of course, it goes much further than that. Everything the horse does is proof positive that this horse is the smartest, most beautiful, most loving, most athletic, and most talented animal to have ever graced the planet.

I believe horsepeople are *born* horsepeople. It's not their fault. You must learn to accept your horsegirl for what she is, because you can't change her and you can't just kick her out of the house. Besides, experience has taught us that she won't leave anyway.

Our One-Horse Family

The briefest period in the history of our family was the One-Horse Era. It could have been measured in hours. It began when we signed the lease papers for Sincerely Yours, an eleven-year-old Arabian/Quarter horse mix. The era ended when the unstoppable force we called "Jamie" collided with the unmovable object we labeled "Hiliary." It had to do with a wheelbarrow full of manure. If the wheelbarrow had the ability and desire to empty itself, this conflict could have been easily avoided.

Of course, The Great Wheelbarrow Debate was merely a symptom of a deeper problem. Astonishingly, both girls wanted control of Sincerely Yours. Both were eager to implement their own ideas regarding horse care and handling. About the only thing they agreed on was that the other should be absent:

"Mom! Jamie won't share Sin Boy with me!"

"She won't share? Listen, you two are giving me a headache."

"His name is *Sincerely Yours*, Hiliary," Jamie reminded her.

"I call him *Sin Boy*."

"He is Sincerely Yours," Jamie insisted.

"Sincerely mine? Okay! You can leave now."

"No, Hiliary. You have to call him Sincerely Yours."

"Alright. I'll call him Sincerely Mine."

Jenny had had enough: "In a minute, he's going to be *Sincerely Nobody's*. Now, how are we going to resolve this?"

"I can't share a horse with her," Jamie said. "I end up doing *all* of the work."

"I do the work," Hiliary insisted. "You just go back and do it over again."

"There's a good reason for that little sister."

Hiliary saw an opportunity, "Mom, why can't I have a horse of my own?"

"Because, Hiliary, your dad doesn't want us to have even *one* horse."

"So?" said Hiliary.

"So?" said Jamie.

"So," said Jenny as she pulled a small newspaper clipping from her purse, "we'll just have to leave this taped to his beer."

It was a picture and a description of an Arabian gelding. Above the picture it said "FOR SALE." Below the description Jenny had written: "For Peace in Our Time."

CHAPTER 3:

Nature of the Species: Big, Fast, Beautiful, and No Longer On The Menu

As a parent of a horse-crazed adolescent female, it behooves you to study the evolution and nature of the equine species. By doing so, you will understand *why* the horse stomped on your foot and broke it in three places. You'll discover *what* the horse was thinking when it kicked you in the knee for no reason. You will learn *whom* the horse is really running away from when it's time to come in from the field at night. You will learn *when* to give up the chase and *how* a *cold six-pack* makes it all seem okay.

The Horse Gets Around

Horses were not always the big, beautiful creatures we know. Their evolutionary ancestor, *Eohippus,* was about the size of a dog and is universally regarded as "ill-featured" (ugly). *Eohippus* first appeared in North America about sixty million years ago. Ten million years later, boredom and a lack of ground work drove him across the land bridge from Alaska into Asia. From Asia, the horse spread throughout the Eurasian landmass and into North Africa. This is an example of what can happen when you don't have good fencing.

When *Eohippus* left our continent, he created The Great Irony of Horse History – when North America had horses, it had no people, and when it had people, it had no horses. This would change, of course. And it would cost horse parents a lot of money.

Through eons of evolution and general walking about, the horse grew in size and strength. By the time the Europeans set off to colonize the New World, the horse had only a vague resemblance to ugly little *Eohippus.* By that time, horses were so good looking, the Europeans decided to take a few with them. By doing so, they reintroduced the horse to the Western Hemisphere and thus completed the gigantic circle started by *Eohippus,* fifty million years ago. And we've been riding them in circles ever since.

Domestication of the Horse

No one can say for sure who first came up with the idea of riding horses, but I'm willing to bet it was an eleven-year-old girl. Indeed, the discovery of prehistoric cave paintings depicting young females curled up asleep with their horses have convinced experts that the horse disease was prevalent in Early Girl. The unearthing of ancient pottery etched with the 4-H logo and the "EAT. SLEEP. RIDE." motto seems to support this.

The Horse-Human Relationship

Horses often behave in ways that seem peculiar to humans. They seem wary of the most ordinary objects. They startle at the slightest provocation. They resist the simplest procedures. They act like they don't trust us.

It's true. Horses have an instinctive distrust of our species. The reason for this is simple: a million years ago, our species ate their species. Not all of them, but it was enough to notice. And they've held a grudge ever since.

Humans have been trying to make up for this little indiscretion for the last ten thousand years. Now we want to be *friends* with horses. We want them to *like* us. Well, forget it. Our inexcusable behavior has turned the horse into Nature's Most Emotionally Damaged Species. What were we thinking?

(Shhh...It's the Horse Whisperers...)

Lucky for us, there is a small group of men and women who really, really, understand the equine species. These people get plenty to eat and thus pose no threat to horses. Horses sense this and walk up to these men and women like they've known each other for years. These people are called "Horse Whisperers," but nobody knows why. These gentle, caring people are very sensitive and the rest of us are dirt.

Today, the quiet, reclusive Horse Whisperers can be found in blockbuster movies, on TV talk shows, in best-selling books (including works of fiction, non-fiction and a new category: non-fiction with lots of fiction in it), at expensive seminars, and on the glossy covers of national magazines. They have a great deal to teach us.

A Creature of Flight

A horse's main defense against attackers is his ability to run. While he is capable of punishing an assailant with a well placed, swift kick, it is his ability to outrun his pursuers that has allowed him to survive and evolve. When a horse bolts for no apparent reason, it's probably because he's looking for a head start.

A horse's wariness of anything new or different is an essential aspect of his "flight, not fight" character. "Run or be eaten," Nature says. "Be afraid of everything," Nature adds. "The new guy bringing your grain is not to be trusted," Nature blathers on. Nature is like a nagging little demon perched on the horse's head, whispering instructions of dread and trepidation.

While the purpose of training is to overcome these natural inclinations, even the most thorough training by the most able handlers cannot eliminate a horse's essential nature. Horses will always retain a degree of unpredictability. In fact, they can be downright sneaky. Do you remember the beer commercial where they kicked the extra point instead of going for two? Surprised everybody.

Other Physical Attributes

In addition to speed, the horse is blessed with several other physical attributes that promote survival. Since many of these affect the animal's handling and care, kids and parents need to be aware of them. Or, if you want, when something goes wrong, you can simply ignore all this and blame it on the horse. "He's just acting stupid," you can say.

Vision

Horses have excellent peripheral vision. This is because their eyes are located on the sides of their head. The best place to hide from a horse is directly in front of him. This is also a good way to get knocked on your rear.

Because of the horse's superb peripheral vision, it is difficult for predators to sneak up on them. This has to be terribly frustrating for the predator. He works all day, stalking with cunning, and just before he springs his trap – BOOM – the horse takes off. Heck, that horse *knew* that ol' coyote was in the bushes all along. Horses always know "there's something in the bushes" – whether there is or not.

Hearing

Like most targets of predation, the horse has an acute sense of hearing. This allows him to detect predators while at a safe distance. It also enables him to hear you fixing your breakfast while he waits in his stall for his morning grain. At this point, he will likely test *your* hearing.

Sleeping

It is commonly known that horses, like members of the U.S. Supreme Court, are able to sleep while standing up. Horses have the unique ability to lock their legs in a resting position and are perfectly comfortable like this for long periods of time. This readies the animal to make a quick get away in case the owner wants to give little cousin Sarah a pony ride.

Adult horses require a minimum of two hours of REM sleep a night. During these periods, horses lie down just like you and I do. Well, mostly on their sides, actually. They don't do well on their backs, since all four legs would be sticking up in the air. Occasionally, a wide-awake horse will lie down to sun itself or roll around in the dirt. This behavior is typically witnessed following a bath the night before a horse show.

Breathing

Have you ever looked at a horse's nostrils? They're huge, aren't they? Did you ever ask yourself why they're so big? Or don't you care? It's okay if you don't. Most of us have never given this a second thought. It doesn't mean that we're bad people. And it doesn't mean that you're a bad person. So don't worry about it. You can live a happy, productive life without ever knowing why a horse has big nostrils. I know I have.

Ears

You can tell a lot about a horse's temperament by watching his ears. If his ears are constantly moving, the horse is probably nervous. If there is no ear motion, the horse may be slow or lazy. This is my kind of horse. I like the ones who, at some point in their lives, just sort of decided "Aw, to hell with it..."

If a horse lays its ears straight back on its head, it can indicate displeasure or downright orneriness. You may finally learn for yourself why they say, "Watch out for the back legs."

When a horse has his ears up at about a 45-degree angle, it indicates a calm, but alert condition. The horse is actually conniving against you. When you see this, prepare to be outsmarted at any moment. These are the ones that get away from you.

Teeth

A traditional method of determining a horse's age involves examining its teeth. I'm not really sure how this works. I've looked in a horse's mouth and – you know – so what? One time, I even tried counting its teeth. But since my main objective was to come out of the horse's mouth with the same number of fingers I went in with, the count was hurried (onetwothreefourfive...) and very likely inaccurate.

Legs

A horse's forelegs have no skeletal attachment to its trunk. Their shoulder blades are held in place by muscles. This enables the animal to withstand the constant, rigorous pounding of regular long-distance retreats. However, this anatomical feature limits the horse's ability to move his forelimbs outward from his body. Since our arms are fully attached, we humans do this easily. It must seem completely unnatural to the horses when they see us do it. You can almost hear them saying: *Oh geez, it really grosses me out when you guys do that.* Just another thing for horses to worry about.

Intelligence

How smart are horses? Expert opinion varies, but most observers put them someplace between an eggplant and a dog.

I kind of go back and forth on the issue. I know that horses are not the intellectual heavyweights of the mammal class, but to me they usually look like they know what they're doing. So, normally, I give them credit for being reasonably intelligent. That is, until I see one gnawing on a fence post. But then, I think, perhaps he's just bored or having dental problems.

Then I see the same horse with his foot caught in a water bucket. But, you know, maybe something spooked him. It could happen to any horse.

But then I come across the same horse and the same bucket, and this time it's stuck over his head. Maybe it's just having a bad day.

Oh, brother, he keeps running into the stall wall.

Okay, this one really is an idiot.

CHAPTER 4:

Buying A Horse:
Caveats and Carrots

Buying your first horse is like getting married. It's a beautiful experience, but living together afterwards kind of ruins it. If you're not careful, what begins as an exciting new adventure can quickly become a painfully expensive ordeal.

Don't allow your kid to rush you into buying just any old horse. She might be in a big hurry, but you don't want to waste time and money on a bad match. Take your time and avoid making hasty decisions. Take *lots* of time. If you're smart, you can stretch the process out over several years. By then the child may have her driver's license or be married and have kids or be retired.

A Failed Strategy

Of course, you have to remember with whom you're dealing. I tried Delay and Stall tactics with Hiliary. Like a true horsegirl, she was prepared for it:

"Dad, since its Saturday, can we go look for a horse?"

"Hiliary, you're not old enough to have your own horse."

"But, Dad! I'll be thirty-two next month!"

"No, you won't. You'll be ten."

"Yeah, but you're trying to wait until I'm thirty-two."

"No, I'm not."

"Yes, you are! You're trying to make me wait until I'm older. You think I won't like horses anymore. You think I'll like boys and not horses."

"That's not true, honey!"

"Mom said it might be a good idea."

"You're mother is hopelessly insane."

"So you want Jamie and me to keep sharing Sin Boy? Or would you rather have peace in our time?"

"What's that supposed to mean?"

"We can do this the hard way or we can do it the easy way. You know I'm gonna get a horse anyway. So why make things hard on yourself? I'll get the keys."

She had a point. While she wasn't quite ready for the responsibilities of having a horse, I was completely unprepared for her *not* to have one.

Older vs. Younger

There are a number of characteristics you need to look for in your child's first horse. To begin with, the horse needs to be calm. For this reason, many parents prefer their younger children to have an older horse. Experienced horses are more apt to be calm and steady and more tolerant of a youngster's mistakes. Some horses are so laid back that they are described as "bomb proof." Nothing bothers them, and they are impossible to startle. It's because these horses are dead. And since they are no longer upright, your short-legged tyke will have no trouble mounting them.

Manners

Another thing to consider is the horse's manners. Yes, horses have manners. Or at least they should. You don't want to buy a horse that tries to kick or bite when you groom him. You want one that's easy to catch and easy to lead around. Like a properly trained husband.

Size

Make sure the horse is big enough for your kid. Your daughter won't win too many blue ribbons if her feet are dragging on the ground. I know smaller horses look safer, but don't let that fool you. Ponies can be downright mean. They like to bite and kick. When I see a pony, I think of Moe from the Three Stooges. If ponies had fingers, they would attempt to poke you in the eyes and yank on your ears.

A horse can be too big, as well. The problem with big horses is awareness – on the horse's part. If you stick a fifty-pound, eight-year-old girl on a ¾-ton, 18-hand giant, the horse will forget she's there. *Why doesn't anybody ever ride me?* he'll think.

Sex

At some point in your search, you will have to consider the question of sex. Of course, as an adult, you can go that route, but most horse sellers would prefer to be paid by check or cash.

Training

If you buy a horse that is not broke, you soon will be. Hospital bills, fence repairs, doctor visits, and lawsuits make a mockery of family budgets.

On the other hand, you don't want a horse that's been trained to death. In the first place, these animals are not cheap. It takes a great deal of time, knowledge, and effort to train a horse. This isn't included for free. Besides, you don't want a horse that has more education than you have. There's nothing more annoying then a know-it-all gelding.

Conformation

Make sure that the prospective horse has *good conformation.* Be absolutely certain about this. Nothing is as important as good conformation. It is vital that the horse has good conformation and not bad conformation. I just wish I knew what it meant. But I don't have the slightest idea. No one does.

Reading a Classified Ad

Horses for sale can be found in the classified ad of your local newspaper or in regional and national equine publications. To the beginner, these ads may be a bit confusing. For example, many people do not know what "Obo" means. Isn't it obvious? Obo is clearly the horse's name. Obo is the most popular horse name in the United States. A quick review of the classifieds will reveal hundreds of horses with that name.

The ad will contain basic information such as breed, size, age, color, price, training, and show experience. From this you should be able to determine whether or not it's worth calling for further information. However, use caution when reading these ads; some sellers resort to bizarre sales tactics or make fantastic claims regarding the horse's abilities. For example, I once saw an ad that ended with what seemed to be a threat on the horse's life, "Willing to sacrifice, $5,500." Another claimed, "Will geld, if desired." This is absurd. Why give the horse a choice? And finally, one ad stated the horse "goes in parade." *Big deal,* I say! *They ALL go in the parade.* I've seen 'em do it. That's why they have clowns coming up behind with wheelbarrows.

Sometimes, classified ads for horses look more like men looking for female companionship. I know it sounds crazy, but after reading these, what would you think?

"Handsome and athletic hunter. Great disposition. Green, but willing attitude with flashy front action. Possible stud material." OR...

"Big, powerful, no vices but completely broke. Easy keeper. Will drive. Easy breeder, real lover. Likes cattle."

Buyer Beware

In spite of what you may have heard, people who sell horses are not just out to rip you off. This is far from true. The fact is, they'd be just as happy to rip off someone else.

You need to be careful. Don't be afraid to ask questions. For example, here are some questions I like to ask when looking at a horse:

1. Do you have any beer in the house?
2. Is it cold?
3. Can I have some?

Often, a novice buyer will attempt to fool the seller into thinking he or she is an experienced horseperson. It never works. This is due to the Rule of One. The Rule of One states: *No matter how many intelligent, relevant questions an inexperienced buyer asks, it only takes ONE stupid comment to blow his or her cover.*

Example: You thoroughly examine the animal from head to tail. You make appropriate grunting noises of approval or disapproval at the right places. At the end of the inspection you ask something like "Has she been gelded?"

Do not try to hide from your ignorance. It will find you.

Viewing the Horse

If you wish to view the horse, start by having the seller lead the horse out of the barn or the field. Have the owner stand the horse sideways and check out his teeth. Look at his head, shoulders, and buttocks. Ask if he's been castrated. If he checks out okay, begin looking at the horse.

Make sure that all the parts of the horse are connected. You don't want to spend your time and money on a horse with missing or incorrectly attached parts. Examine the horse's back. The croup should be about the same height as the withers. If you don't know where these parts are, simply ask yourself this question: "Does this horse look like fat people have been riding him?"

Forelegs should be present. The hooves should be in good proportion to the size of the horse and not on backwards. The horse should have a nice big butt. All good horses have nice big butts. Check the animal's teeth and no matter what you see, say "Oh, *man!*" several times. If the tail is too low, ask what can be done about this. Beware of the large, dish-shaped head. That's a sign of one too many fights with the fence post.

The Test Ride

Never buy a horse without riding it first. At least make your kid ride it. Some sellers use tranquilizers on the horse before offering it for a test ride. Make sure you find out if the seller did that. If so, ask for a couple. You may need them.

The Wind Up...

Once your child is riding around by herself, the seller will approach you. He'll say something like "They look great together" or "Your daughter is a good little rider." You'll reply, "How kind of you to say so, considering she is being dragged on the ground with her foot still in the stirrup."

...and The Pitch

The seller is now ready to make the pitch. He usually starts by listing all the horse's relatives going back at least fourteen generations:

"His father was the great El Ferno Khamal who sired over a hundred national super-duper show champions. His mother was the sister of the aunt of the cousin of the grandmother of the horse owned by the lady who lived next door to the famous stallion, Wind Dasher, who used to jump the fence and...well, I'm sure you've heard of him ..."

You haven't, but the cascade of names continues:

"...and his great grandfather was Hesa Financial Disaster who sired the...blah, blah, blah...and the great Brighton Beach who sired Hesa Son of Beach and...blah, blah, blah...his second cousin was the famous Itsa Three-Eyed Monster who once trailered past the site where Secretariat is buried...blah, blah, blah..."

Then you get to hear of the horses many accomplishments:

"Yup, this horse has been trained at the Snobbury Hills Facility in Virginia and is a Registered National Show Horse. He won twenty-three blue ribbons at the National Championship Show in '96 and was the Reserve Champion of the Universe in '98 and he can drive a car."

Closing the Deal

At some point, the seller will attempt to close the deal. He'll begin by asking a question such as "Well, what do you think?" or "Do you like him?" This is a polite way of saying, "Let's get this over." If you hesitate in committing yourself, the seller may warn you that "other people" have expressed interest in this horse.

Yeah, Right

Sure, EVERYBODY wants THIS horse. The whole damn country is going stark raving mad over him. People are queuing up all over the United States and Canada just to have a peek at his picture. There have even been reports of rioting. News of this impending sale has had a profound effect on Wall Street. And Monty Roberts called.

Leave

Tell the seller, "We'll get back to you." Pluck your kid off the ground, dust her off, and get out of there.

A Failed Strategy, Part 2

"Dad! Mom! Ohmigod. That's the horse I *have* to have!"

"But Hiliary, that horse bucked you off and dragged you around with your foot in the stirrup! He didn't even try to stop."

"He's SO perfect! I want him!"

"You're not ready for a horse like that! Don't you get it?"

"When can we pick him up, Mom?"

"Hiliary, that's the first horse we've looked at. Don't you think..."

"Did you give the guy a check, Dad? He's absolutely perfect."

"We need to look at a few other horses before we make a -"

"I'm gonna need a saddle. I hope you brought enough money for some new reins. And a good halter too."

"Hiliary, we are not buying that horse."

"Dad. Dad, Dad, Dad. Why do you torture yourself like this?"

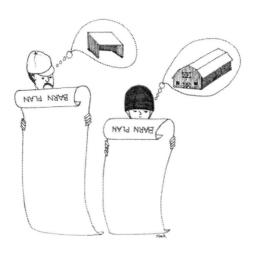

CHAPTER 5:

Housing the Horse - Barns, Loans, and Holes

One of the most important considerations of horse ownership is where you will keep the animal. As a parent, you have to be careful. If you do not set limits, you will soon find yourself selling everything and moving to the country. Here, you must live without city water, without city sewer, without shopping centers and – Heaven forbid – without cable Internet access.

Do not underestimate the potential of this hazard. You MUST set limits and you MUST stick to them. You gotta be tough. Just let them know it's never going to happen. I've been there. And now I'm *here*.

How I Got Here

When Jamie and Hiliary first asked for a horse, I told them no, forget it. I was very firm.

Shortly after they got the horse, the girls asked if they could show him. I forbid it, I said. I was quite clear.

After their first show, the girls decided sharing a horse wasn't working. They needed another one. Not gonna happen, I told them. I was adamant.

His name was Bruiser. And now that we had two horses, Jamie and Hiliary felt it was time for a horse trailer. Absolutely not, I said. I put my foot down.

My foot came down on the accelerator of a 1986 Ford half-ton pickup truck. We had to buy the truck because we needed something to pull our brand new Honolulu blue and silver horse trailer. I got to pick the color.

Finally, when they suggested we move to the country so the horses could be at home with us, I drew the line. This was out of the question. I wasn't going to sell our suburban home and uproot our family for the sake of their horses. No way. Not an option.

I kind of like it out here.

Boarding the Horse

Okay, so I failed. But YOU don't need to. Because when YOU say *no*, by gosh, that's the way it's going to be. So... just what are you going to do with this horse that you said you'd never buy in a million billion years? Well, don't worry, you don't have to get a place in the country in order to keep him. You can keep him at a local boarding barn. For now, anyway.

If you choose to keep the horse at a boarding barn, visit several of them before making a final decision. You need to do your homework. Like anything that has to do with horses, searching for the right boarding barn is a complex and time-consuming process. If you do it properly, it should take approximately six years before you find the one that's just right.

First, wander around the inside of the barn. If you find yourself bashing your head every few steps, this may be a sign of low ceilings. Beware, a barn with low ceilings can suffer from poor ventilation. A barn with higher ceilings has better ventilation and you will need the additional vertical space when they hand you your first month's boarding bill.

Everybody knows that a good barn does not smell bad. So be alert for any unusually unpleasant odors. However, don't go overboard on this. Remember it's a barn, not a church.

Check out the tack room. The tack room should be the most civilized part of the facility. It's the only place in the entire barn where you can set down a cup of coffee and not have it teeming with straw bits and barn bugs in less than two minutes. Since you will be storing valuable equipment here (beer, cigarettes, lighter, potato chips), it should be clean and dry. It should smell like leather and have plenty of room to hang the whips and chains. Some people like the tack room *too* much.

Look in the stalls. Walk in the stalls and stay for a while. Spend the night! All stalls should be big enough to allow a horse to turn around. The act of turning around is the closest thing horses have to an indoor hobby, and it would be cruel to take that away from them.

Take a look at the land surrounding the barn. Is there an area for riding? Is there room for your kid to fall off her horse? Can an ambulance get there easily? Are there trails nearby, just in case going in constant circles drives your child insane or dizzy?

This may seem like a lot of effort. Well, it is. But consider how much time and effort you would spend looking for an apartment for *yourself*. Because that's exactly what you'll be doing if you pick the wrong boarding barn for your daughter's horse.

A Horse at Home

While boarding has its advantages, there is nothing like having your horse right at home. However, before I describe the virtues of the horse at home, I need to warn you about something: never, under any circumstances, allow the girl to bring the horse into the house. I know, it seems obvious. I shouldn't have to say it. But in a society where hair dryers come with instructions like "Do not use while sleeping" and the box for a string of Christmas lights tells you "For indoor or outdoor use only" and a warning label on a camera says, "This camera only works when there is film inside," I felt I should say something. The horse will not appreciate being inside and no good will come of it. It never has at our house.

Having the horse at home not only saves boarding costs, but also provides your youngster with the opportunity to take care of the horse herself. This is a big responsibility. It helps build character and promotes maturity. However, it could kill the horse. Make sure that your child or someone in your family has a clue of what she or he is doing.

Keeping a horse at home allows the bond between the child and the horse to grow quickly. Horses pay attention to who's being nice to them and who's not. If the girl feeds, grooms and exercises the horse and gives it love and attention, the horse will learn to trust her. However, sometimes the girl spoils her horse so badly that he resents anyone else taking care of him:

"Jamie, I think Eddie hates me."

"Why do you say that, Dad?"

"It's obvious! Just look at the way his ears are pinned back."

"Um...Dad? You have his halter over the top of them."

"Well...I see...Yeah, I guess he has an excuse this time... He *does* hate me, you know."

"He doesn't hate you."

"Then why does he always pin his ears when I go into his stall? He doesn't do that with you."

"It's because I take care of him most of the time. And he's a momma's boy. He's just spoiled, that's all. With you, it's more of a territorial thing."

"I don't *want* his territory. He *poops* in his territory. What's he protecting?"

"It's just an inherited behavior, Dad. Think how you would feel if Eddie showed up in our living room?"

"Yeah...I guess you've got a point..."

"Yeah. Mom probably wouldn't like it either, would she?"

..."Jamie?"

"Yes?"

"You aren't planning anything, are you?"

Why Can't We All Just Get A Loan?

If you are a horse owner and you're lucky, you already live out in the country and own some acreage. If not, you may have to move. Or you may need to build a barn. Some people build the barn themselves. These people are known as "masochists." The rest of us pay to have this done. We're known as "In Debt."

Whether you build the barn yourself or hire somebody to do it, you may need to borrow money. Loans for construction purposes are very different from regular mortgage loans. The main difference is that the bank actually expects you to read the documents you sign. That's where I got tripped up. So, read the following section very carefully. Pay particular attention to any small print, large print and/or words in italics. And don't forget to sign your name next to each and every "X."

My Loan Story

Soon after we moved to the country, I went to a local bank to see about securing a loan for building our barn. I thought all I'd have to do was look at some papers, pretend to understand them, and sign my name a few times.

The bank had other ideas. The loan officer, a kind and helpful lady, informed me that I would have to take out a "construction loan." This was fine with me. I smiled and asked where I should sign.

The Loan Lady smiled back. But it wasn't a regular I'm-Happy-To-Be-Alive-And- Serving-The-Public kind of smile. It was more like a I-Deal-With-Idiots-Like-You-All-Day-Long smile. She hauled a monstrous form out of her desk and plopped it in front of me. Across the top were the words SWORN STATEMENT. She informed me that I could sign on back of the statement, but only after completing the front.

I didn't want to complete the front. The front scared me. The thing was at least a hundred lines long and it had a dozen columns. The columns included headings like "Description of Work or Material" and "Original Contract Amount" and "Adjusted Contract Amount" and "Total Retention Withheld" and "Labor Compensated But Withheld Due to Original Contract Amount Adjusted by Retention." I felt insignificant.

The front side also included a good deal of small print. It read like this:

*"That the following is a complete statement of each contractor, supplier and laborer for which laborer the payment of...*blah, blah, blah...*That (he) (she) has not employed or procured material from...*blah, blah, blah...*That (he) (she) makes the foregoing statement as the (owner) (contractor) (subcontractor) for the purpose of representing to the owner or lessee of the aforementioned (this), (that), (and the other thing)...*blah, blah, blah...blah"

This was clearly the work of a group of Insane Devil Lawyers. And I didn't want anything to do with it. (Me) (Myself) (And I) tried to explain to the (Loan Lady) (Bank Employee) (Troublemaker) that all this legal stuff was giving me (a headache), (indigestion), (gas). I just wanted to build a stupid barn.

As I struggled to complete this S.O.B., I made a few sworn statements of my own.

In the end, I was amazed at how fast the bank people worked. It took them a mere five days to plow my SWORN STATEMENT through eight layers of financial bureaucracy and provide me with a check for the contractor. However, it took the contractor only four days to build the barn. Day Five proved to be rather awkward for both the contractor and me. A day late and ten thousand dollars short.

43

The barn got built and the contractor got paid. And I couldn't have done it without the help of dozens of hard working and dedicated employees of the financial community. I really liked 'em. I sent a note inviting them all over to help build my fence.

Holes

If you're serious about keeping the horses at home, then you better get serious about digging some holes. Digging holes is the single most important thing a horse parent can do. Without holes, you couldn't have fence posts. Without fence posts, you couldn't have fences. Without fences, you couldn't have a real pasture for the horses. And without a real pasture, the horses would eventually wander off and look for a better life. This would upset adolescent horse-crazed girls everywhere and they would riot.

Digging holes is hard work, so it's kind of nice to think of something else while you're doing it. I like to pretend I'm one of those early pioneers who came west to tame the land. Pioneers were a hardy folk and they weren't afraid of facing the hardships of a hostile environment. They took nature head-on and taught it a lesson.

The problem with taming the land is that the land has a way of taming you back. While you won't have to deal with any backbreaking tree stumps or fend off packs of wild wolves, you may be confronted – depending on where you live – with the most dreaded enemy of all hole diggers – clay.

Clay can kill. Unlike regular dirt, clay takes exception to being dug. It likes where it is and resents being put somewhere else. It's thick and heavy and slippery. You can't get much on the posthole digger and what you do get has a tendency to slip back into the hole. You end up going after the same bit of clay over and over again. Clay is evil.

The Fence

If you plan on building your fence out of good ol' wood, be prepared to pay out a lot of good ol' cash. You will need hard lumber for your fencing, like oak or hard pine. If you use an inexpensive, soft type of wood, the horses will mistake the fence for chewing gum and proceed to eat their way out. Remember, these animals do not think ahead.

Because of its relatively low cost and because it's easy to work with, many people prefer electric wire fencing. The most important thing here is to make sure the fence is properly grounded. A poorly grounded fence will have a weak current and this allows the horses to get away with way too much. In order to test if the fence is receiving enough current, simply instruct one of the neighborhood kids to place his or her hand firmly on the wire. Sorry, but you'll have to use a different kid each time.

Horse Crap

The handling and disposal of manure is another important aspect of keeping the horses at home. At first, it won't seem like a big problem. Believe me, this one will sneak up on you. The average horse produces between thirty and forty pounds of manure a day.

With that level of production, the little innocuous pile will soon grow to an impressive size. It will develop an identity and personality all its own. Thick green grass will sprout from its top and little white things will appear all over what might be considered its face. Its appetite for space will become voracious. It will consume your entire back yard. You will attempt to pile it higher and deeper, but this only helps for a while. The sprawl will continue. Eventually it will threaten your barn, your out buildings, and even your house. Resistance is futile. You are about to be assimilated.

What can you do? Most horse care guides will tell you something incredibly helpful like, "You need to have a means of disposing of it." No kidding. This is typically followed by a reference to what most sober observers regard as a mythical figure: The Gardener Who Wants All Of Your Manure For Fertilizer So Badly That He'll Come And Get It And Pay You For It. Now, don't get all excited. This person is as real as the Blair Witch. People love talking about him, but no one has ever seen him.

CHAPTER 6:

The Drudgery of Daily Care

Caring for a horse is a huge responsibility. Doing it properly takes time, effort, and money. And then some more money. Long before we bought our first horse, a local horsewoman explained the realities of ownership to my daughters, "It's just like marriage, girls. Getting one is easy and doesn't have to cost much. But keeping him can be pretty darn expensive and time consuming – whether or not you actually use him."

That last part bothered me. I'm still not sure what she meant. But my wife and the girls didn't seem to have a problem with it, so I just left it alone. However, I did understand that "pretty darn expensive" actually meant "pretty darn expensive for your parents." Local horsewomen love spending other people's money.

How Much?

Most experts who write articles addressing the cost of daily horse care shy away from providing the reader with any concrete dollar figures. The reason for this, they say, is that prices vary from region to region and over time. Thus, they run the risk of being inaccurate or out of date. This is a shame. There is no reason to be vague, because there is nothing difficult about determining how much money you need for routine horse maintenance. It's easy! You simply set an absolute limit to the amount you are willing to spend and then multiply by two. Or three.

Eating

Drive past any field of horses and chances are they will look as if somebody nailed their faces to the ground. This is a horse's favorite posture. Standing up, neck extended downward, lips pressed to the turf. Tails swishing. Total contentment.

They're eating. It's what horses live for. I'm not sure how this species propagates itself. It's a wonder they stop eating long enough to breed. Wild horses, for example, spend up to sixteen hours a day eating. They eat a lot and they take their time about it. They eat more slowly than cows, for instance. Cows, of course, have very busy schedules, and they tend to feel guilty if they spend more than eight hours a day eating. Horses are not quite the go-getters cows are.

Since domesticated horses are our prisoners, *we* have control over their eating habits. *We* choose when the horses eat according to what is convenient for *us*. *We* are the ones who bring the hay. *We* are the ones who mix the grain. *We* are the ones who decide when to let them out to the field to graze. And *we* are the ones who have to pay the vet bill when our horse colics, because *we* have totally ignored the fact that horses have natural eating patterns for a reason and not adhering to them has totally screwed up their digestion.

Hay

An average horse consumes between three and four tons of hay a year. It is the primary source of food for a horse. Hay provides the bulk roughage necessary to allow the horse to perform its principal function in life: making manure. This in turn provides the caregiver with her primary task: mucking stalls. Mucking is the word horsepeople use for the act of removing horse crap from the animal's stall. It's a fun word.

Hay is packed in units called *loaves*. Each *loaf* weighs exactly a helluva lot. They are held together by *twinder vines*, a product of Canada. In order to access the *loaves*, the *twinder vines* must be *cliffed* (cut) using a *rasker tool.* This allows the *loaf* to be subdivided into identically measured sections called *slices*. These may be fed individually or in pairs. *Slices* come in three different flavors with their own names: grass hay (Timothy), grain hay (Jim) or legume (Ed).

How much hay should you feed your horse? Opinion varies, but experts agree that whatever you're doing now is wrong. Mainly they say, "It depends on a lot of things."

Grain

Horses need grain for energy. They love it and will knock you over to get at it. They should have some every day. How much grain should you give your horse? Experts suggest that you "not feed them too much or too little."

Horses sometimes consume wheat bran. Wheat bran should be familiar to those of you who back in the early eighties believed it was fashionably healthy to eat sawdust.

Grain mixed with molasses is called sweet feed. When you pour on milk it becomes a breakfast cereal for people at $4.27 a box. It's good!

What kind of grain should you feed your horses? Experts say, "Well, it could be a combination of many things."

Water

Have you ever watched a horse eat a whole apple? What did you see? He slobbered all over the place, didn't he? Of course he did. It's because horses have an unbelievable amount of spit in their mouths. They drool like idiots. And this is the main reason I think Mr. Ed the Talking Horse was unrealistic. The voice of a real talking horse wouldn't have that resonant quality of Mr. Ed's speech. Instead, he would probably sound more like Daffy Duck: *Thuffern' thuckatath! I'm a sthompin' sthud sthtallion! Perhapths I thould get you thumb towelths?* Result: equine saliva all over Wilbur's face.

Spit is very important to a horse. It's crucial to their digestive process. In order to digest their food properly, they need to produce at least ten gallons of spit a day. It takes a lot of water to make that much spit. Are you giving your horse enough water? Experts say you aren't.

Supplements

There is a multitude of commercially available supplements and vitamins for horses. These include products that make their coats shinier, things to help 'em poop, things to help pass sand, things to help keep flies away, things to help them see better, to hear better, to feel better, to smell better, to taste better (in Texas and Japan, at least).

Experts agree that supplements and vitamins may or may not be helpful to your horse.

Digestion

Horses are one of nature's most impressive physical specimens. They enjoy several advantages over humans.

They're bigger than we are. They're stronger than we are. They're faster than we are. However, there are a few things we can easily do that a horse can't. For one thing, we can puke. And we do it with such ease and grace. A horse has a real hard time doing this. And when they do, it comes out their nose. Also, people are capable of breathing through their mouths. Horses can't. And finally, if we swallow something bad, we can cough it back up. Ever see a horse do that? Without a doubt, we are the master species.

How is any of this relevant to a horse's digestion, you ask? Well, it's like this: when a horse swallows something, it STAYS swallowed. This means if he eats something that's difficult to digest, it just kind of hangs around in the stomach, which is already quite small to start with. Anything that goes into a horse's stomach needs to think about leaving as soon as possible to make room for the next batch of whatever. If it doesn't, the horse is headed for a heap of trouble.

Unlike humans with our World Famous Gastric Juices, a horse's digestion depends upon a group of friendly bacteria that reside in the cecum and great colon. These affable organisms celebrate life with great gusto - as long as the horse is eating. They sing, dance, ho-dee-hoe and breed while they merrily breakdown into usable material the contents of what the horse ate. The presence of these friendly bacteria is why horses can eat hay and we can't. However, if the horse is fed improperly or at the wrong times, this joyful little community becomes hungry and depressed and eventually dies off. It's really sad.

Exercise

Horses are not lazy animals. They love physical activity. They run for any reason or for no reason. But a horse's favorite reason to run is the simple joy of watching slightly overweight, middle-aged men on the verge of cardiac arrest stumble around the paddock attempting to catch the horse and put a halter on him.

In the wild, horses get plenty of exercise just by being horses. They stampede up and down the canyons and prairies for no other reason than because they can. One minute they're all grazing peacefully and the next they're running like hell. It usually starts when one horse notices another horse moving a bit too quickly. This makes him think that the moving horse saw something, so *he* starts moving. Others sense the movement of the first two and a chain reaction takes place. Soon the entire herd is running like the dickens for absolutely no reason at all. After a bit they realize "Oh, silly us" and the stampede gradually comes to halt. And they all get a good chuckle out of the episode. Then a hungry mountain lion pounces on one of them.

Domesticated horses will stampede when there are enough of them in a pasture together. But instead of five or six miles in one direction, they have to settle for going around in circles several dozen times. This means they have to pass the perceived danger spot many times, but that doesn't seem to matter. They're running, and that's all nature has instructed them to do. They're not required to display any intelligence. Nonetheless, it's good exercise.

If you happen to keep your horses in a place where there is not a great deal of room to run in the pasture, you will need to exercise them manually. This involves a process known as *lunging*. Here, you attach the horse to a long line, stand in the middle of a round pen or other appropriate area and then make him run around you. Actually, *lunging* is not a good term for this practice. It could easily be confused with *lounging*. And that's not something horses are specifically trained to do.

Grooming

All horses need daily grooming. The grooming process begins with picking out the horse's hooves. Here you will find mud, manure, a squashed frog, small stones, a very bad smell, and a very good reason not to own horses. In order to perform this task, you have to lift the horse's leg. This is very difficult, but it can be done. All you have to do is place one hand above the horse's knee and one below it, then ease his leg into the air by applying gentle pressure below the knee. Use your third hand to do the actual picking.

Brushing the horse's coat is another important aspect of grooming. Brushing should be done vigorously, except in sensitive areas. You know what I'm talking about. Make sure you allow ample time for brushing. Experts say a proper brushing takes approximately eighteen hours a day.

Don't forget to clip errant hairs on the horse's nostrils, face, and legs. Horses hate this and they often attempt to kick the person doing the clipping. Experts say you should stand at least ten feet from the horse while clipping him. This is physically impossible, of course. But don't let that discourage you.

Mucking Stalls

Maintaining a clean living area for the horse is essential. For most new owners, mucking is regarded as the most disgusting aspect of horse ownership. This is because most new owners have not been introduced to the REALLY revolting tasks such as hoof-picking, sheath cleaning, and taking rectal temperatures. On the overall Gross-Out Scale, mucking barely makes the chart.

This is not to suggest that mucking is a simple job. Far from it. There's more to this chore than just flipping a few of those round things into a wheelbarrow. An entire technical science lies behind effective mucking. Good mucking involves getting rid of manure and other unwanted material without removing large portions of unsoiled bedding. And this requires High Science.

For most muckers, the tool of choice is the muck rake. The muck rake is scientifically designed to scoop up the round things while sifting out the dry sawdust or wood shavings. The individual tines on a muck rake are scientifically spaced at three-quarters of an inch. As the mucker shakes the muck rake in a scientific manner, the bedding material falls between the tines, while the round things scientifically remain on the rake. These are then deposited into the wheelbarrow. There they will sit for three days or until the owner of the property asks the horse caregiver, "When do you plan on emptying that damn thing?"

Some people enjoy mucking horse stalls. They say it's relaxing. They say it helps them think. They say it's good for the soul. Stay far away from these people.

Another notable phenomenon of mucking science is the *pee spot*. Apparently many horses prefer to urinate in only one or two places in their stall. This is amazing. I mean, who would have ever thought a horse could be that organized? But it's true.

The *pee spot* must be removed daily. Once you find it, it's not hard to get rid of. But finding it is extremely difficult. For most of my mucking career (I retired from the chore in 1996 after Clinton got re-elected – I'd had enough), I simply refused to believe the *pee spot* even existed. Jamie insisted that it did and often reprimanded me for my refusal to address the problem. "My horse is not a pig!" she liked to say.

"Then do it yourself!" I liked to say.

Our inability to see eye to eye during the *Great Pee Spot Controversy* led to many bitter moments between my daughter and me.

A Parent's Role

I know the biggest question you have regarding daily horse care is how much extra work it means for you. At least that was the biggest question I had. I know, we think we're all so tough and if the kids want horses, then by gosh they're gonna get out there and do the work. Because we're not gonna do it. Right?...Right?...HEY, RIGHT?

Experienced horse parents know the truth. Do not be ashamed to admit it. Every parent who has been dumb enough to allow his or her kid to have a horse has done his or her share of barn work. It's just the natural order of things.

I resisted this for as long as I could. When Jamie and Hiliary got their first horse, I drove them to the boarding barn so they could do their horse thing, but refused to even get out of the car. I was in denial. *This isn't happening*, I told myself. *It's not real. All I have to do is sit in this car, they will come back, and then we can go home. And I don't have to do anything.*

But this was like falling asleep at the beach during low tide and thinking you're going to wake up dry. It happens like this:

"Please hold my horse for minute, will ya, Dad?"

"Well...okay. I guess that wouldn't be too hard."

Then:

"Can you walk him around a little while I muck his stall?"

"Oh...I suppose."

"And we need some sawdust."

"Um..."

"But the wheelbarrow is full of manure. You have to empty it before you get the sawdust."

"Listen, I'm not here to..."

"Will you hold him while I put his saddle on?"

"But..."

"Will you get his saddle for me? It's in the tack room. Get his grain while you're in there, will you?"

"I...you...I'm not..."

"And a couple flakes of hay."

"What?"

"Get the bale on top. You'll have to cut the binder twines first. The scissors are hanging on the door. Next to his water bucket. Bring that too. You have to fill it first."

"This is not my..."

"Make sure you check the hay for mold. Tear the flake apart a little and then..."

This can go on for hours, if you let it. So don't let it. The key is to set limits. Yes, you want to help your kids and be involved with what they're doing, but you don't want them to take advantage of you. Be up front about it. Make sure she clearly understands there are limits to what you're willing to do.

For example, if she wants you to haul water, explain that you will haul only two buckets at time. If she wants you to *lunge* her horse, tell her okay, but only around in circles. If she wants you to buy, load, and unload three hundred bales of hay, say that you'll do it, but only during the week or on weekends. If she wants you to build a brand-new barn with fourteen stalls, tell her ten stalls is ALL she'll get. You've *got* to be tough.

Handling the Horses

After all this time, I'm still not particularly good with the horses. Even when attempting the simplest tasks, I'm awkward, tentative, and extremely unskilled. And the horses know it. Their reactions range from taking advantage of me (e.g., sneaking bites of grass as I attempt to lead them from the barn to the pasture) to simple tolerance (e.g., standing patiently while I fumble around putting their halters on – sideways, upside down, inside out, hopelessly twisted) to actually performing the procedure themselves (forcing their face and head through the proper openings of the halter so that all I have to do is latch it).

Despite all of this, the horses and I get along pretty well. They have learned not to expect too much from me, and they display an astounding degree of patience with my overall ineptitude. They give each other these looks and roll their eyes sometimes, but experts agree, that's normal.

CHAPTER 7:

The Sick Truth of Horse Health

Horses have a reputation as one of God's most healthy creations. They're big, they're strong, they're fast. They have regular bowel movements. How could such a magnificent creature bc considered anything but a prime example of animal kingdom vitality?

It's easy. Just own one. If you take care of horses for any length of time, you'll discover an unpleasant truth; they're sick. Or if they're not now, they will be.

The list of potential equine ailments, maladies, and diseases is long and ugly. As a parent, you have to deal with the fact that whatever is wrong with the horse, it's your fault. At least, you will have to pay for it.

What Can Go Wrong

What can go wrong? The list reads like something out of the Book of Job:

Actinobacillus equuli, vesicular stomatitis, socialism, acute equine respiratory syndrome, acute face syndrome, sore foot, Trypanosomiasis, Infectious Malectious, African Horse Sickness, Hard Sunday Disease, Surra, bad breath, Simbu virus, Salmonellosis, Special Prosecutor's Disease, strangles, laminitis, heaves, hoes, howdies, equine Protozoal Myelitis, Can't Load/Won't Load Sickness, Rabies, Anthrax, Metallica, Korn, Botulism, Pessimism, Clostridium perfringens, Fringensper diumclostri, Friggen H, Corn Popp'n Disease, Cryptosporidium, dourine, don'turine, equine encephalomyelitis, The Encyclopedia Britannia, Don't Got No Thumb Complaint, equine influenza, equine Morbillivirus, Close-In Disease, Far-

Away Syndrome, equine viral arthritis, Leptospirosis, PHF, EHV-1, EHV-4, EPM, HMO, REM, WWF, NATO, and IRS.
And that's just the beginning.

Colic

Perhaps you noticed the list does not include colic. That's because colic is so special, it deserves its own section. Colic is its own list.

Colic is a digestive disorder. It stands out from the pack for one simple reason: its causes. The causes are just about anything. Or nothing. Or everything. A horse can colic from eating the wrong thing or eating too much of the right thing or not enough of the right thing, or from changes in diet or not enough changes in diet, or from emotional /psychological factors, or from a new horse in the stable or an old one leaving, or from being startled, or from not enough sensory stimulation, or because the sun came up, or because it's Tuesday. Maybe it's raining.

How do you know when a horse has colic? If he acts like a husband with a hangover who lies around on the couch on a sunny Saturday afternoon when the lawn needs to be mowed, this is a sign of colic. And what should you do? Treat the horse *exactly* like you would the husband, get him up and moving as soon as possible. Do whatever it takes. Get a rope and walk him around if you have to.

Do not ignore any symptoms that indicate colic. A bad case of colic can be extremely serious. The mere mention of the word "colic" carries a great deal of psychological weight with anyone who has ever dealt with a severe case. It's kind of like the word "FIRE!" *Anyone* can say it and *no one* should ignore it. No matter what time of night it is. Or how cold it is. Or if you're eating supper. Horsegirls know this:

"DAD! You *have* to come out to the barn! Right now!"

"..."

"DAD! Wake up! Right now!"

"..."

"Wake up, wake up, wake up!...WAKE UP!"

"...Jamie...Why are you pounding on my door? Do you know it's three a.m.?"

"Eddie has colic!"

"You mean like last week – during Monday Night Football?"

"But he really has it this time!"

"And the week before? You know, when I was in the shower?"

"But..."

"It was 15 degrees outside."

"Mom said you wouldn't mind..."

"I'm not going out there. We'll look at him in the morning."

"Colic, Dad! Colic!"

"..."

"Don't you hear me? I said COLIC!"

"..."

"COLIC! COLIC! COLIC!"

"Ooooookay...I give up. You win. Give me a minute to get my coat and my boots. And my pants. Colic, you say? You win. I give up. I'm just gonna get my coat and my boots. And my gun. Because after I look at your horse, I'm gonna go out behind the barn and shoot myself. You win..."

Calling the Vet

When should you call the vet? Most of the time it's a matter of common sense and you just have to use your best judgment. However, there are at least five emergencies that require you to call a veterinarian immediately. They are:
1. Profuse bleeding.
2. Colic. (COLIC! COLIC! COLIC!)
3. Eye injury.
4. Foaling.
5. Instead of shooting yourself.
6. An inability to stop at five items.
7. Miscellaneous.
8. Others.
9. That's it.
10. Really.

When you call the vet, be prepared to answer three questions:
1. How is the horse's appetite?
2. Is the horse active?
3. Cash, check, or charge?

Vital Signs

The vet may instruct you to obtain the horse's temperature, pulse and respirations or "TPR."

Pulse. The important number to remember for the pulse is "36." That's the number of people in all of recorded history who have successfully taken a horse's pulse. It's not easy.

Respirations. Respirations are a bit easier. Simply watch the number of times the animal breathes in and out in one minute. Some people count for thirty seconds and multiply by two. When they do this, they get "60," but that's wrong. The answer should be "12."

Temperature. Taking a horse's temperature is an unpleasant task. It takes a great deal of courage to start the process. Or even think about it. An inexperienced person should never try to take a horse's temperature. Neither should an experienced person. A horse thermometer is three feet long and you always run the risk of it getting "sucked up." I apologize for any unfortunate mental images this gives you.

If the vet insists it's necessary to take the horse's temperature, then do it properly. This means you'll need at least two, preferably three people. First, make sure everything is tied down. Next, determine who will insert the thermometer. This can be decided by coin flip, drawing straws, or by threat of violence. Secure the thermometer by tying it around the wrist of the unlucky inserter person. Next, tie the unfortunate inserter to the back of a mechanically sound four-wheel drive vehicle. Make sure the vehicle is running. The second person should lift the horse's tail to expose the target area. Remember, "close" does not count. You must achieve a bull's-eye. The third person can serve as witness to the event for posterity or if an insurance claim is necessary.

Resisting the Vet

Some horses resist veterinary care. When this happens, horsegirls often become apprehensive and start to whine about how their horse will react. Not to worry. The vet will simply fasten a metal device around the upper lip and squeeze it. This device is known as a "twitch" and it will help keep them quiet. It can be used on the horse as well.

The twitch releases natural endorphins into the horse's blood stream and this helps calm him. Inexperienced owners may see this and say, "Hey you're hurtin' the horse!" In these cases the vet will often respond by suggesting that the owner immediately take over care of the animal, since they think they're a damn expert or something.

Signaling the Vet

In isolated rural areas, veterinarians are known to make routine rounds of all their customers. Since the vet has to travel long distances and can't stop everywhere, it is traditional for people in need of the vet to tie dishrags on the front gate. This signifies that they want the vet to come and do their dishes.

First Aid

It's not necessary to call the vet for every ailment the horse suffers. If you own a horse, you should be prepared to handle minor emergencies yourself. You'll need an adequately stocked first aid kit. It should include syringes, needles, gloves, bandages, gauze, ointments, colic medicine, and so on. However, in the real world, a typical first aid kit contains such things as an empty bottle of rubbing alcohol, buttons from last year's western riding outfit, straight pins arranged so that they prick your fingers, a dead nine-volt battery, a used Kleenex, a butter knife, lipstick, and a dried up hoof black applicator.

After witnessing my daughter care for a wound on her horse, I have come up with an eight-step wound cleaning process:

1. Stop the bleeding.
2. Blame parent.
3. Clean wound with expensive spray antibiotic.
4. Gag.
5. Dress the wound.
6. Complain bitterly.
7. Protect the wound.
8. Fret about it the rest of the day.

Lids on the Buckets

Many horse care products come in big white buckets. Dietary supplements, digestive aids, constipation remedies, and geriatric horse products all come in big white buckets. But these are not ordinary big white buckets. These are Torture Buckets. A committee of talented sadists spent years addressing the question of how to make opening these buckets as difficult and painful as possible. Their lid design should be considered a scientific marvel. These lids come with specially designed lips that are cemented to the top of the bucket. Around the lid are little tabs that say, "Tear off." "Tear off"..."tear off"..."tear off"..."tear off." On the flip side of these tabs it says, "your finger nails"..."your finger nails"..."your finger nails." Other little tabs are more direct: "Forget it"..."forget it"..."forget it" they read. Some buckets come with useful instructions like "Remove lid before use" or "This product will not harm your horse, but removing the lid will cripple your fingers."

Wormers

Like human parents, horses have parasites. Horse parasites include large and small strongyles, roundworms, pinworms, larvae of botfly, eye of newt, toe of turtle, and butt of bat.

It is important to maintain a worming program for your horse. I know, "Worming Program" sounds like you're *giving* horses worms. Perhaps they ought to call them *Un*worming Programs. Or Worm Out Programs. Or X-Worm Programs. Or Anti-Worm Programs. Wormers come in a variety of brands and flavors with heavy-dose-of-chemical names like Triantisymethocainex or Antitricanosisanoblicaltestrest.

Laxatives

We don't like to talk about it or even think about it, but sometimes horses suffer from constipation. Horses that rarely or never get constipated are known as "good movers."

There is nothing worse than a constipated horse – except for those dangerous first moments as he becomes unconstipated. While many products are useful in preventing or relieving this affliction, none is more powerful than an industrial strength laxative called "STAND CLEAR!" The warning is in the name.

Insecticides and Traps

One of the most pleasurable aspects of owning a horse is the opportunity to kill flies. Horses make manure and flies breed in it. Since horses make tons of manure, flies do tons of breeding. Right now, as you are reading this, thousands and millions of fly fathers and fly mothers are creating and raising thousands and millions of little fly families – right on your property. How does that make you feel?

I don't know about you, but I hate 'em. I REALLY hate 'em. I love killing the little bastards. I want to see them suffer.

My family is concerned. They think I take the whole anti-fly thing too far:

"Dad, you've been out here for three hours. Haven't you killed enough of them?"

"Don't interrupt me, Hiliary. I'm making your barn safe for humanity."

"But the flies just come back when you leave."

"Not ALL of them, kiddo. A whole bunch of them are never going to bother us again. Sweet Annie and I made sure of that."

"*Sweet Annie*? You gave your fly swatter a name?"

"You bet, honey. And we're gonna take this barn back."

"Dad, I think you should go inside now..."

"No matter how long it takes. By the time we're done, these obnoxious little gangsters are gonna wish they were never born. I like ripping off their wings."

"I think I better go get Mom."

"Great idea! She can use Bloody Bertha!"

"Just wait here, Dad."

"Godspeed, Young One! Bring back reinforcements! I'll hold out here!"

"Oooookay, Dad..."

The people who make anti-fly products are just like I am. They *really* hate flies. To them, it's not just a way to make a living; it's a sacred mission. And a hobby. They want flies to die and suffer a lot. The names of their products are proof of this. Some take a cheerful, breezy approach and give their products upbeat, cute names like (these are real products) Bye Fly, Trap & Toss, and Big Stinky. These people love their murderous work. Other names indicate a more hopeful attitude: Fly Relief and Fly Gone. Others have direct, down-to-business names: Fly Kill, Fly X, and Fly Terminator.

Which one should you use? Use them all. Mix them! Remember: KILL! KILL! KILL!

Weighing Your Horse

There may come a time when you will need to know your horse's weight. This information can be useful for such things as measuring out medications, charting a horse's growth, tracking his dietary needs, determining the weight your truck will be expected to tow, or responding to the call of a European meat broker.

How do you determine your horse's weight? Some people measure this or that and divide by some random number and add three hundred and are happy with what they come up with. But you don't need to do that. Instead, use the following tried and true formula and everything will work out just fine: $E=mc^2$.

Treats

Horses love treats. There's one that's called Horse S'Mores. Your horse weighs something. After eating these, he'll weigh s'more.

Farriers

Farriers take care of your horse's feet. To those of you who are new to horses, you might think, well, big deal. Well, it is. Regular visits by a farrier are essential to your horse's health. The only part of a horse's anatomy that needs more attention then his feet is his stomach. Without routine attention, the horse could go lame or have other health problems. As an old farrier saying goes, "No hoof, no horse." Of course, you could say that about *any* part of a horse's body. For example: "No head, no horse." "No neck, no horse." "No stomach, no horse." "No butt, no horse."

Farriers have all kinds of medieval looking hooks and tools. And they use big trucks and ovens. So make sure you pay your bill on time.

Lame Humor

Sometimes a vet or a farrier will make a bad joke about the way a horse is limping. This is known as *lame humor.* Or he will say something like, "Hey, horse, why the *long face*? Heh, heh, heh." Encourage your horse to step on the feet of these individuals.

Equine Dentist

Another important specialist is the equine dentist. This brave expert is also known as the Tooth Farrier. The equine dentist will occasionally pull a horse's tooth if necessary, but usually he performs a treatment known as "floating." Floating sounds like it would be a light and enjoyable procedure. HA! It's a complete misnomer. When an equine dentist floats a horse's teeth, he uses this big-ass file that looks like it came straight from the high school metal shop. These amazing people are able to get this device into the horse's mouth and file its teeth without using drugs! The horses are sedated, however.

You Make Me Feel Like a Natural Horse

There are those who contend that horses would be better off and less sick if allowed to remain in the wild. You know, romping and frolicking in the wilderness, unfettered by human contact. To this, I must reply with all the dignity my tongue can muster: *thhhhhppppp.*

According to statistics that some equine expert compiled or completely made up, horses live much longer and healthier lives if they are domesticated. Some argue that this does not matter. They say all that matters is that horses would be *happier* if left unbroken and out of control, romping around, sowing their seeds, and so on. It's a sweet notion, but reality is harsher than that. Left alone, these poor souls lead pretty rough lives. They get beat up and shot at. They have bad teeth and suffer from poor diets. It's like being a husband or boyfriend of a horse-crazed female during show season.

There is one thing wild horses can do that their domesticated cousins can't: they can breed like rabbits. I'm not sure if this analogy has ever been applied to any species other than humans (and redundantly, to rabbits), but you get the idea. The Wild Horse *has* to reproduce at a higher rate than the Kept Horse in order to make up for the losses suffered from living that nasty, brutish, and short lifestyle.

Art and literature have romanticized the image of wild horses thundering through the valley on some vital mission. Seeing it takes your breath away and such. But a closer picture of individual horses reveals a multitude of injuries and imperfections: an eyeball hanging out of one, another one has an entire hoof missing, three of them are limping, two of them look like walking skeletons. They have all kinds of bruises, abrasions, incisions, lacerations, and punctures. All of this goes untreated, even the sores with pus oozing out of them. It's like looking down on Yugoslavia from twenty thousand feet. You think, *hey what a beautiful country.* But get down to ground level and...oh...

CHAPTER 8:

Riding: Keeping a Horse
Between Her and the Ground

Contrary to popular opinion, humans are not born with an ability to ride horses. Riding is not instinctive, it's not natural, and it's not easy. It hurts.

Images from popular entertainment suggest that riding a horse is simple. In movies, on television, and in cheap novels, any ol' guy hops on any ol' horse and just rides away. No bucking, no rearing, and no falling off.

If you insist on believing movies, television, and cheap novels, go right ahead. You will die. As for me, I'll listen to what the bruises on my backside are telling me.

Once Upon a Horse

For most of my life, I thought all you needed to know about horses was "giddyup" and "whoa." That was before Bruiser.

Bruiser was Hiliary's horse. His name was appropriate. And I did not want to ride him. But Hiliary insisted:

"Aw, c'mon Dad! All the other dads ride horses. Why don't you?"

"It's simple, Hiliary. Bruiser is not equipped with brakes."

"But, Dad ..."

"I'm not getting on your horse, Hiliary."

"But..."

"No."

"DAD! ... If you ride him, I'll let you pretend you're Genghis Khan, Leader of the Mighty Golden Horde and Conqueror of the World!"

"But ..."

"Don't worry, Dad, I'll put a lead line on him and take you around."

For an experienced horseperson, riding your daughter's horse is no big deal. Experienced horsepeople get on easily, they stay on with little effort, and make the whole thing look natural. But it doesn't work that way for the rest of us. We need help getting in the saddle, we have no idea what to do once we're there, and we look – and feel – like idiots the entire time. But then again, how many opportunities does a guy get to be Genghis Khan, Leader of the Golden Horde and Mighty Conqueror of the World?

Bruiser was a good horse, no doubt, but he could not quite get the hang of the up and down thing; when I bounced up in the saddle, he went down. That wasn't so bad. But it meant that when I was going down, *he* was coming up. That was bad. BAMM, BAMM, BAMM. That's how we rode around.

BAMM, BAMM, BAMM. Across the front yard.

BAMM, BAMM, BAMM. Around the cars in the driveway.

BAMM, BAMM, BAMM. Around the house.

BAMM, BAMM, BAMM. Around the house again.

The horse was taking me in circles. I couldn't be upset with him; show horses are trained to go around in circles. He probably thought I was pleased with his performance. He didn't seem to realize that I was Genghis Khan. I tried to give him the cue for "Attack the Huns," but he mistook it for "Run into the fence and knock me off."

I concluded the ride face-to-face with Mother Earth.

Okay, I'm a lousy rider. And taking ANY kind of riding advice from me may seem like getting advice from a divorced marriage counselor or a bankrupt financial planner or a dead health professional. But there is one question I can help you with: "Should you, the parent of horsegirl, feel guilty because you choose not to take part in the riding experience with your daughter?" The answer is "Hell no."

Riding Lessons

Before buying a horse, your child should take riding lessons. The goal of riding lessons is to eliminate the kid's bad riding habits before bad riding habits eliminate the kid. A trained professional should be contacted.

The preferred instructor must know his or her business, have years of experience with different breeds, enjoy working with kids, have a great deal of patience, and most important of all, be willing to work cheaply. Free would be best.

It's important that the instructor assess your child's riding history prior to the first lesson. It will not do for an instructor to simply throw your little lamb chop on the horse and say, "Okay, let's see what ya got, kid." If your darling has some riding experience, the instructor may want to skip the first few lessons such as "How to Get On A Horse and Face the Same Direction the Horse Is Facing."

Riding lessons are typically short. This is because they involve a great deal of work for the horse and because most kids have a short attention span. Some lessons last as little as 15 minutes. Or even 10. Heck, I've seen them over within 30 seconds.

If your little honeybun shows any progress after a few lessons (or even if she doesn't), the instructor will initiate the next level of training. This consists primarily of brainwashing. Your little pollywog will be hypnotized into thinking it's a natural, constitutional, God-given right for each and every American girl to have her OWN horse. It's easy! And your parents won't mind at all! In fact, they'll like the idea!

All right. Okay. If that's the way it's going to be, then make sure your little warthog gets lessons in basic horse care. This should include feeding, grooming, exercise and mucking stalls. Unless YOU look forward to doing these activities.

Additional Professional Assistance

You may find it necessary to seek the help of other professionals. These include a nurse, a paramedic, a priest and a lawyer. And a bartender. Consult the Yellow Pages.

Tack

Proper riding requires proper equipment. The term for riding equipment is *tack*. Think of *tack* as the stuff that holds your kid on the horse.

Tack has a terminology of its own. To non-horsepeople, *tackspeak* sounds like a foreign language. But don't bother trying to learn it. I'm convinced that horsepeople make most of it up as they go along.

When confronted with a heavy dose of tackspeak that involves spending money, an effective response can go one of two ways. If you hear:

"Dad! We absolutely need to buy a tiebolt and chainblock so that I can get the girth spanner between Eddie's narrows. The torque bit is too rough on his poll-dock!" You can respond in kind:

"Jamie, I would like to do that, but the accrued balance of our value-added credit line does not permit a fiscal re-expansion. We must delimit and rollback all current monetary outlays."

Or if you hear:

"Dad! Eddie needs a new spit-dorfer so that I can use a lap brace with a martinspeck. His latch holder is worn out!" You can offer a bold but vague denial:

"You're wrong, Jamie. You're just dead wrong."

Safety First

As in any activity that combines large, unpredictable, incredibly strong animals with small, unpredictable, incredibly senseless kids, horseback riding has an element of danger. You must take precautions.

Horses are heavy. They look heavy and they feel heavy, especially when they're standing on your foot. Most experts believe that a horse will not intentionally step on your foot. They claim that a horse's little brain is completely occupied with the whereabouts of his *own* four feet, and he can't be concerned with where other individuals choose to put *their* body parts.

Two other behaviors to be on guard for are biting and kicking. Again, experts agree that when a horse bites, he doesn't really mean it. "It's just a reaction to environmental stimuli or something," they like to say. Experts also like to say such things as "It must be a human's fault" and "People don't have horse problems, horses have people problems" and "Humans are evil."

Safety Equipment for Riders

While all parents should be concerned about riding safety, the primary role of Safety Nazi usually falls to the mother. It's not that the fathers don't give a rip. It's just that mothers pay closer attention to this sort of thing. Most experts believe that there is a genetic link to safety awareness behavior. Like mothers in the animal kingdom, human mothers have been conditioned by evolution to nurture their young and keep them from harm until the little one is old enough to fend for itself. Meanwhile, the father's primary role within the family unit is to go out and gather beer.

The difference between the male and female approach to safety can be seen in the equipment that each deems necessary for riding. If a child asks to ride her horse, a father is likely to respond by asking, "Do you have a hat? You should wear a hat." A mother on the other hand will have a whole list of required safety wear, such as a WWII GI style combat helmet, an NHL approved goalie mask, chain mail, cast iron breastplate, Siberian winter boots with steel toes, and a complete set of bumper pads.

Around our house, the use of safety equipment has always been a subject of great controversy. Jenny and Hiliary have had this conversation 783 times:

"Hiliary, don't even *think* about getting on that horse without your helmet."

"But, Mom, I don't want that stupid helmet."

"It's not stupid. And it will help protect you from a serious head injury."

"How can putting on that stupid ol' helmet protect me?"

"It's simple Hiliary. If you don't put it on, *I'm* going to hurt you."

"*Mom!*"

"Do you want to end up like your Dad?"

"You mean like when he puts his boots on the wrong feet?"

"Yes."

"And when he calls you by the dog's name?"

"Yes."

"And when he thinks I'm Tiger Woods?"

"Yes."

"Better get my helmet."

Show Ring Riding

The show ring looms large in the life of a young horsegirl. It looms so large that I have devoted an entire chapter to it.

In essence, this type of riding requires weeks and months of preparation, and an entire day or more of participation for approximately eleven minutes of actual riding time.

Trail Riding

For pure, simple enjoyment of the riding experience, it's hard to beat good old-fashioned trail riding. This is an activity the rider and the horse can enjoy together almost anytime. However, since trail riding requires only basic equipment, it can be done at a fraction of the cost it takes to show a horse. This is simply not acceptable to the average horsegirl.

Long Distance Riding

Only experienced riders should attempt long distance trail riding. This type of riding can last several days or even weeks. It can be combined with other outdoor activities such as camping and fishing and getting lost. Some people even hunt on horseback. You can commune with nature, experience its simple joys, and then kill something.

Normally, long distance riding takes a great deal of planning and preparation. If you want to do it right (i.e., live through it), you really need to know what you're doing. However, some long distance riding involves absolutely no planning by the rider. The horse makes all the decisions. He decides when the ride will take place. He also determines the direction, speed, and destination. The rider's job is to hold on and hope the horse gets tired.

Dressage

Dressage is the ancient art of horsemanship. Its roots go all the way back to the Greek master Xenophon (pronounced "Bill"). The techniques and philosophy of dressage were handed down through the ages to other

Europeans. The word dressage is French in origin and means literally, "to torture with boredom." It is perhaps the most mispronounced word in equestrian history (hint: it rhymes with corsage).

According to the dictionary, dressage is "the execution by a horse of complex maneuvers in response to barely perceptible movements of a rider's hands, legs and weight." At the Olympic or Grand Prix level (be careful, some people don't like it when you mispronounce "Prix"), these movements include French-sounding terms such as *piaffe* and *pirouette* and *passage* (rhymes with corsage again). At your little cupcake's level, they include *le straight line* and *le round circle*.

Of course dressage is much more than a set of complex movements, bewildering patterns, and imported French phrases. It's actually an entire philosophy. For proof of this, ask any true dressage advocate to sum up what dressage is all about in a short sentence. She can't. She can't even do it in a couple of paragraphs. She'll eventually just give up and hand you a book. Or write one and hand it to you. I think it's kind of like quantum physics.

Western versus English

There are two main styles of riding: western and English. It's relatively simple to tell them apart. Western style riders look like cowboys. English riders look like they're prepared to kill a fox.

Another main difference is the style of the saddle. The western saddle looks exactly the way you've seen them in John Wayne movies. It's big, heavy, and has a horn. An English saddle looks like a western saddle that the makers forgot to finish, but shipped anyway. "Where's the rest of it?" you might say upon seeing one for the first time.

Gaits

In between "giddyup" and "whoa" a horse does many things. Or not.

The manner and speed that a horse moves is referred to as a "gait." There are several types of gaits:

Walk. The walk has been defined as "a four-beat lateral gait." Oh, come on. I knew exactly what walking was until I came across this definition. "Four-beat lateral gate?" This sounds like the animal has been trained to jazz dance sideways or something. I think it would be more helpful just to imagine the horse moving along to the tune of *Old Grey Mare.*

Trot. Webster insists a trot is nothing more than a "moderately fast gait of a quadruped in which the legs move in diagonal pairs." I think of a trot as a "moderately fast gait of a four-legged beast designed to make a two-legged rider look like an idiot."

Canter. A canter is an "English controlled three-beat combination gait with much suspension following the third beat." Also available in French and Spanish.

Gallop. Like the walk, a gallop is a four-beat gait. However, there isn't any of that "lateral" nonsense in galloping. This is the Straight From Point A to Point B in a Big Hurry type of gait. *William Tell Overture* kind of stuff. This is where the horse lets it all hang out; it's where he is at his best. Horses love to gallop, and riders who are lucky enough to arrive at Point B still on the horse like it too.

Jog. This is the western version of the trot. It's slower. Much slower. Sometimes it's so slow, you wonder if the horse is moving at all. In fact, the most talented horses are capable of jogging in place. But so what?

Lope. I like "lope." I mean the word itself. I like the way it looks on paper. And I like the way it sounds. I like saying it. Lope, lope, lope! Lope. It's a good word.

Riding horses isn't for everybody. To do it properly takes time and dedication. In order to have a safe, enjoyable riding experience, you need to learn how to control your horse and to deal with problems as they arise. It also helps if your groin and buttocks are made of iron.

CHAPTER 9:

Horse Sex

There is no way around it. If you're kids are involved with horses long enough, sooner or later you're going to have to deal with the subject of horse sex. The direct approach works best. Simply sit your kids down, look them in the eye, and ask them to explain it to you. Unless you grew up on a farm or have strange tastes to begin with, the details of this subject are probably a mystery to you.

How Horsegirls Solve Problems

I have nothing against sex. In fact, it's how I was started. And given the right circumstances and species, I'm rather fond of the whole idea. But there are some aspects of horse sexuality with which I am not entirely comfortable. For instance, do you know what the word "gelding" means? Do not feel stupid if you don't. I didn't know for a long time. For me, "gelding" was one of those mysterious equine terms I heard bandied about the household. It was part of that verbal background noise a new horseparent often hears but has no hope of comprehending. It went right along with terms like "snaffle bit" and "withers" and "crippling personal debt."

I remember the day I discovered the meaning of "gelding." It was a stunning epiphany for me. In an instant, I grasped the cruel essence of our short, brutish existence. And I'll never be the same (although I'm still better off than those poor geldings).

The truth was revealed to me while I was driving my daughters, Jamie (age 15 at the time), Hiliary (age 10), and their friend Andrea (age 16) to a horse show. In the course of their conversation, they used the term "gelding" several times. Unwilling to remain in the dark, I broke in:

"Girls, what exactly does 'gelding' mean?"

Silence. Then giggling.

I repeated the question.

"You really don't know, Dad?" Jamie snickered.

"Lemme tell him!" Hiliary piped in.

"Yeah, let Hiliary tell him," Andrea said.

"Okay, Hiliary," I said. "Tell me what it means."

She told me.

Again, silence. I watched her face to see if she was serious. And what I saw was profoundly disturbing: Hiliary was beaming. From ear to ear. And for the first time in my life, I was terrified of my daughter.

"No, they don't," I finally muttered.

"Yes, they do!" Hiliary insisted. "They do it to *boy* horses!"

"Why? Why would they do this?"

"It makes the horse calmer and easier to control," Jamie explained.

"I bet it does! No trouble understanding that. Really shows 'em who's boss. They're probably thinking, *My God, what next?*"

"Umm ... Dad? There's something else you need to know."

"You might as well say it, Jamie. What could be worse?"

"Mom already knows about this."

I guess this gives us a pretty good idea of what kind of world we would live in if horsegirls ran it.

Differences in Genders

The gelding procedure brings the number of horse genders up to three: the mare (female), the stallion (male), and the gelding (confused). While every horse is an individual and has his, her, or its own personality, each of the genders has certain general characteristics.

Mares are typically more trusting. They will also exhibit maternal instincts. What good this does the rider, I have no idea. I suppose in right circumstances, it could even cause trouble. When a mare is in heat, she is grumpy and unpredictable, and she can make life miserable. For us, anyway.

The geldings are less trusting (for obvious reasons), but are generally more reliable and emotionally stable and make wonderful interior decorators. However, for some riders "there's just something about them that's missing."

The stallion will display more energy and spirit than their gelded brothers. They have so much more to live for. Also, stallions will do things that geldings would never dream of. For example, they drink beer, smoke cigars, and leave their dirty socks and underwear all over their stalls.

Breeding

As a simple horseparent, you really don't need to become an expert on the subject of horse breeding. In fact, I can assure you that you don't *want* to become an expert on horse breeding. I've witnessed this procedure and believe me, you really don't want any part of it. At least you shouldn't want any part of it. However, you should be aware of the basics. If the subject ever comes up, you don't want to look like a complete idiot.

Horse breeding is accomplished either through artificial insemination or something called "live cover breeding." Like Internet romances, artificial insemination can occur without the subjects ever meeting or seeing one another. The advantages to this arrangement are obvious: no first date jitters, no superficial attitudes regarding appearance, and no performance anxieties. However, unlike Internet romances, artificial insemination requires that one partner actually be male and the other actually be female. No room for deception here.

Live cover breeding requires the presence of both partners. It also takes some preparatory work. First, the breeder must assess the mare. This includes collecting such vital information as the age of the mare, her physical dimensions, foaling history, regular cycling pattern, and history of infections. A good example for all you single guys and gals out there.

If the horse is a maiden mare, the breeder must first apologize to her and then have a veterinarian palpate her (the horse). I'm not exactly sure what this involves and I don't think I want to ever learn. Let's just drop it.

Prior to the actual Deed, the breeder typically engages in a process known as "teasing." Teasing is a kind of formal introduction. It involves leading the mare up to the stallion (with a fence in between them in order to maintain good propriety) to see if she shows signs of heat. Names are exchanged at this time, as well.

During the teasing process, the stallion will do everything he can think of to impress the mare. He struts about with his head and ears up high. He arches his tail, and grunts and squeals. He stomps his feet, wrings his neck, and generally acts like a fool. If the mare is not in heat, she will squeal and stomp right back at the stallion. This is her way of communicating to the stud that she has a headache. Some mares are so offended by these unwanted advances that they actually spin around and attempt to kick the stallion. This behavior is known as "Equine P.M.S." (Pretty Mad at the Stallion).

If the mare is in heat, she will display a more passive attitude. If she likes the stallion, she will simply stand there and gaze at him with a stupid look in her eyes. Kind of like how Angela looks at Brad now that the babies are coming.

Live cover breeding can be dangerous. The handlers must be prepared for a thing called "stallion exuberance." By the time the breeders are ready to start the process, the old boy will probably have a good idea of what is going on and may decide he no longer needs human assistance. An unprepared handler may find himself being unceremoniously dragged to the breeding shed. And when the stallion gets to the shed, there damn well better be a mare waiting and ready for him. If not, the handlers are in for a different kind of trouble.

There is no need for me to go into further details regarding this subject. Use your imagination or consult the Internet.

CHAPTER 10:

The Truck and the Trailer -
The Budget Busters

Here is an example of what technology has done for the human race. Less than a hundred years ago, horses served as our primary source of transportation. After the turn of the century, the automobile or "horseless carriage" made its debut. The mass production of this amazing invention meant that we no longer had to rely on our equine friends to get around. Cars were faster and more convenient. Technology was making things easier for us and the future was bright.

Then came the horse trailer. At first, horse trailers were considered a luxury. Only two kinds people owned them: the rich and those involved in some aspect of the horse business. The rest of us managed to live happy and productive lives without them.

In time, mass production techniques made the horse trailer available to the average person. This had profound implications for the human-horse relationship. The widespread use of horse trailers allowed for one of the most radical role reversals in history: instead of relying on the horse as a means of transportation, we are now responsible for providing *them* with a ride.

We're always bragging about how intelligent we are in relation to other animals. If you ask me, the horse trailer is a perfect example of why we should avoid bringing up the subject.

The Trailer

There are four basic trailer designs. Which one you choose depends entirely on your particular needs and how much money you're willing to throw away. The first type, the *manger* style, is the kind where the horses ride with their chests against the front of a permanent manger. The major drawback to this style – at least for me – is the tendency to confuse the word *manger* with the word *manager*. People ask me what kind of trailer I have and I'll say something like, "I have a *manager* type of trailer" or "I prefer the *manager* style so I can put grain on top of the *manager*." That pretty much ends the conversation.

Another potential drawback to the manger style is that it doesn't leave much room up front. Horses need a little room in the trailer to help keep their balance while the rig is in motion. Some horses actually get their legs stuck in the manger. I've seen this happen and it's not pretty. In fact, it's kind of bizarre (although it's less bizarre than a horse getting its legs stuck in a manager).

Jamie's horse, Eddie, once got his legs stuck in the manger. "My horse is stuck in the trailer! My horse is stuck in the trailer!" she sobbed. All I could do was stand there and scratch my head while Eddie looked at me with wide, white eyes. If he could talk, I'm sure he would have said something like "Just – just – just...JUST GET ME THE HELL OUT OF HERE!" We did and he was fine. But I think it embarrassed him because he never did it again.

The second type is the *thoroughbred* trailer. *Thoroughbred!* Sounds *fast*, doesn't it? But they aren't. The only thing fast about them is the speed with which they wipe out your checkbook balance. They're just wider and taller than a normal trailer. Horses appreciate this additional space because it alleviates a bit of the "metal coffin" feeling. Some thoroughbred trailers are large enough to include human quarters (and sometimes even a WHOLE human) for sleeping and whatever. If the horses say it's okay.

The third type is the *stock* trailer. This is the "no-frills" option – the "Old Milwaukee" of horse trailers. You know, decent, functional, relatively inexpensive, and surprise winner of that taste test a few years back.

The stock trailer is basically an open box. It has a roof and everything, but a good portion of the side and rear are open to the air. This provides better ventilation and light and horses are partial to that sort of thing. Space, ventilation, and light: make the experience as similar to standing in a field as possible and the horses are happy.

The last type of trailer is the *slant load*. The slant load trailer resembles the thoroughbred trailer, except that the horses ride at an angle facing left. The slant load includes swing partitions that allow the horse to enter from one side and exit the other. It's all very complicated. Horses who use this kind of trailer are easily identified at horse shows; they're the ones that never seem comfortable standing in a straight line.

The Pre-Purchase Inspection

After choosing a trailer style that has the dimension and specifications you desire, it's time to inspect individual trailers. This takes a long time. You need to check for structural integrity, feel for rough spots in the interior, operate all doors and windows, check the undercarriage and springs, test the footing, examine padding, check all exterior surfaces, and test the ramp. Finally, ask the dealer for a test haul. This is not easy to arrange because by now it's 3 a.m. and you'll have to find out where the guy lives and wake him up.

After the test haul, it's time to make some demands. Demand six-ply tires! Demand electric brakes! Demand a weight-distributing hitch! Demand a sway bar! Demand a breakaway kit! And most important of all, demand to know what these things are! Because you don't have a clue!

You should also check for potential problem areas. In general, poorly constructed trailers are noisy and bouncy. Horses hate that. But I think they're being a little unfair. I mean, it's okay for them to give *us* a bone jarring ride, but don't even *think* about doing it to *them*.

Ventilation and airflow are critical factors. However, avoid a trailer with gaps in the floor. Not only does this allow deadly exhaust fumes into the trailer, it also allows urine and manure to escape through the bottom. While this may sound like a good deal, it isn't. Most state police take a dim view of horse manure and pee falling on their highways. Unless you're ready to become a participating member of the Adopt a Freeway That You Will Clean Up Program, avoid this practice.

A good floor is vital for a horse trailer. That thing the Flintstones do in their cars isn't realistic. So don't expect it from your horse. Look for floor braces that run the width of the trailer. Braces every two feet indicate high quality construction. Braces every foot indicate designer compulsiveness. And braces less than every foot indicate a high likelihood of psychosis. Leave as soon as possible.

Pre-Trip Inspection

Prior to every trip, you should perform an inspection of the trailer. First, you need to test the trailer lights and turn signals. Here you must consider the all-important question: "Do the lights work?" The all-important answer is "No." Horse trailer lights never work. Not all of them at once anyway. For example, you may get the right-hand turn signal to work properly, but forget about the left. Turning that on will mysteriously trigger your electric brakes. And perhaps the interior lights work just fine, but the outside running lights perform like they're at a disco party. Cool, but not functional.

So what *should* you do about this? It's obvious, isn't it? You fix 'em! But what *will* you do about this? Nothing. And why? Because you don't know how. Besides, you have two tons of impatient horse flesh packed in the back of that trailer, and it took you an hour and a half to get them in there and they are kicking the be-jeebies out of the side of the trailer, and it's WAY past time to leave. So, to heck with it. Go.

Testing the lights is only one part of your pre-trip inspection. You also need to check the tire pressure, clean and lubricate the exterior, test the brakes, check your road emergency equipment, and examine the spare tire. Next, put your horses away and go inside the house because by the time you get all this done the weekend will be over. *CSI* is on.

Handling the Trailer

Any veteran horseperson will tell you it takes a little experience before you become comfortable towing a horse trailer. They are lying. Unless you drink, you will never be comfortable towing a horse trailer.

While you may never be comfortable, you will get better. It's a lot like bowling. The critical points in handling a truck/trailer combination are starting, stopping, and cornering. The key is to start slowly, gradually building up speed while gently urging the truck and trailer along. Be mindful of the precious cargo you have loaded in the back. Be even more mindful of the little girl sitting next to you. If you do something stupid and the horses get hurt, she will destroy you.

You must remember that sooner or later, you will have to stop. Plan ahead. Start stopping long before you actually have to stop. Once you start stopping you should continue stopping until you actually stop. At this point stop stopping.

The rule of thumb for stopping distance is to allow ten feet per mile an hour when the trailer is empty. This figure increases if you're loaded. It increases even more if the trailer is loaded. Thus, as a safety precaution, I recommend traveling only when the trailer is empty. And don't let any whiny horsegirl talk you out of this. Safety first!

Take corners slowly and evenly without sudden braking. And if you're a guy, don't intentionally go over the curb because you think it's funny. However, if you do happen to take a curb, claim you did it intentionally because you think it's funny.

Avoid sudden and unexpected lane changes. While this adds a great deal of variety and excitement to an otherwise dull trip, a female passenger may assault you with her fists.

Backing

Going forward is easy. Going backward takes a pro. Actually, it takes more than a real pro – it takes *magic*. It's not a skill. It has nothing to do with technique or practice or hand/eye coordination. Backing a trailer is a mysterious Black Art. Only the most powerful witches are truly capable of properly backing a horse trailer. I know this for a fact, because I've seen them do it.

The Black Art of Backing is governed by a set of physical principles found nowhere else in the universe. It is necessary to think illogically. To be precise, you have to think backwards. This is why women are often superior trailer backers; they come by this stuff naturally.

This is how it works: in order to make the back of the trailer turn one direction, you must turn the steering wheel of the tow vehicle in the *opposite* direction. In order to go left you must turn right.

I know what you're thinking. You're thinking, *That's not so bad. Anybody can remember that.* And it's true – to a point. But simply because you turn the wheel in the opposite direction, does not mean the trailer will go in the other opposite direction. It all depends on where the wheels started. If they started too far in one direction, you have to turn them far enough in the opposite of the opposite direction in order to make them go the way you want. If you don't, the trailer will keep turning the wrong way, but not as much the wrong way if you hadn't started turning it the other way in the first place. When you see this happen you say to yourself, *Oh, stupid me! I turned the wheel the wrong way!* So you crank it back the other way.

Surprise! The back of the trailer in now going even further the wrong way. Okay. So what do you do now? You get out of the truck and take a look. What good does this do? Nothing! But you just had to see it for yourself. Back in the truck, you become even more determined to beat this thing. You slow down. Hmmm...you try to think logically. You ponder the rules of cause and effect. Hmmm...

Stop it! Just stop it! Thinking logically WILL NOT WORK. Keep it up and you'll jackknife the thing and all your neighbors will gather and snicker. At this point you realize it's all your wife's (or husband's) fault. A beer sounds good.

The Truck

Once you've obtained a decent horse trailer, you've won half the battle. Now you need a truck. Without a truck, the trailer will sit there dumb and useless with low self-esteem.

Trucks are not like they used to be. Unlike their rugged, hardworking forefathers, who looked with contempt upon anything that smacked of riding comfort, today's trucks often include all the amenities associated with prissy-butt passenger cars. It is not uncommon for a new truck to come equipped with such non-essentials as air conditioning, electric windows and locks, am/fm stereos, cruise control, heaters, and brakes.

Don't be fooled. The new trucks are capable of doing everything the older trucks could do and more. They just *feel* like passenger cars. They hold *beverages.* They're like a half-car, half-truck schizoid mutant or something.

A Man's First Truck

Whether or not it's horse related, a guy's first truck is a milestone. I remember looking for our first truck. All I wanted was a mechanically sound vehicle within our price range. Actually this did not take me long to find. And all I had to do next was to figure out how to peel off the Tonka label.

After a great deal of research and negotiation, I found a truck that had an engine and could make its own noises. When I brought it home, everyone was excited. Jenny said that I got a good deal, and Jamie and Hiliary wanted to go for a ride. The cats tried to chase it out of the yard.

If you have watched enough truck commercials, you know that a truck is supposed to symbolize the male ideal of rugged independence. The idea is simple: buy a truck and you will be "like a rock." To be sure, something DID happen to me when I bought that truck. It happened at the bank. It's called going into debt. Rock-like men pay an 8.5 percent annual fixed interest rate with ten percent down.

How Much Truck Do You Need?

There is an ongoing debate over how big a truck you need to pull horses. One group – we will call them the minimalists – believes you should only buy what you need in order to get the job done. They suggest that in order to pull a typical two-horse trailer, all you should need is a vehicle that weighs 3700 lbs., has a wheelbase of 114", a 6-cyl/4.9-liter engine and a rear axle ratio of 3.5 to 1. The second group – we will call them the "Get A Big-Assed Truck" group or the "Tim Allen School" – agree that if you meet these specs, you won't have any problems – if you're pulling two dogs in a wagon. Those are sissy specs, they say.

Signs of Trouble

Once you find a truck that meets your towing requirements, the next step is to make sure it's in good condition. You are going to ask a lot from your truck and you don't want one that's going to break down on your first trip like mine did. Here are some warning signs of an unsound vehicle:
- bed gaps
- poor alignment
- shot suspension
- flat seats
- hose and belt cracks

- drooping or twisted bumpers

If you see all of these things, then you are looking at my truck.

Numbers and Letters That Can Help You

Like horse trailers, trucks have a lot of numbers and letters associated with them. One useful set of letters is the "GVWR." GVWR stands for Gross Vehicle Weight Rating. This rating is the maximum amount your vehicle weighs with a full tank of gas, passengers, their gear, and some "American-sized" people. Big deal, you say. Well, not so fast, smarty. If you take your GVWR and subtract the "cargo weight rating" found in your owner's guide, you can determine the weight of your vehicle! NOW you can say "big deal."

Another set of numbers and letters is the Vehicle Identification Number, or VIN. The VIN is your truck's real name. All in caps, too. Like:

WI9839EE09041I873948T9803R893R000008BS50294R.

WI9839EE09041I873948T9803R893R000008BS50294 R is not just a pretty name with no practical function. Unlike human names like Jim or Sue, which say very little about the person, a VIN is packed with useful information. For example, the number "39" in a VIN indicates the vehicle's rear axle has a 3.55 ratio. And the letter "H" means it has a 5.8-liter, 351 V-8 engine. It's true! All the numbers and letters in a VIN actually indicate specific information about the vehicle. Pretty cool, huh?

I know what you're thinking. Like any other rational, practical-minded person, you're thinking, "How the hell can you tell which numbers mean what?" Well, you can't. The VIN is like a super-secret code. Sure, it's full of information, but it's impossible to use it in a meaningful way. Sort of like this book.

CHAPTER 11:

Horse Shows: An American Family Surrenders to the Absurd

The horse show is an American institution created by people who belong in an institution. Of all the ideas in the history of our great nation, spending huge sums of money for the purpose of coercing a large, reluctant animal into a metal box and then transporting it long distances in order to ride it in circles has to be the hardest to explain.

Of course, your child can enjoy her horse without horse shows. But thanks to 4-H and other subversive organizations, your daughter will at some point really, really, really, really, really, really want to show her horse. Really.

If you are new to the horse scene, the idea of "showing a horse" may seem like an innocent thing. A couple of hours on a Saturday morning, some friendly "everybody's a winner" competition with blue ribbons and participation certificates handed out at the end. You know, kind of like Field Day at the end of first grade.

Boy, are you in for a surprise.

Horse shows are anything but short and sweet. They are one part picnic, one part beauty pageant, and two parts total war. They incite powerful female instincts for intragender rivalry and conflict. They bring out a primal lust for blood in these high-strung, kick-ass adolescent girls and their hyper-competitive mothers. It's like the first twenty minutes of *Saving Private Ryan* spread out over ten hours. Some will say I exaggerate. But I think horse shows are an example of why some people don't want girls to play contact sports: the boys might get hurt.

Don't get me wrong; I *like* horse shows. I enjoy hanging around horsepeople and observing them with their kids. I miss it if I haven't been to one in a few weeks. But then again, I'm the kind of guy whose favorite part of the movie *Titanic* was when the ship was tipped at a seventy degree angle and the people slid down the deck (wheeeeee!) into the water. Got a chuckle out of that.

Types of Horse Shows

Like any other form of torture, horse shows come in a variety of types. There are small, informal backyard shows put on by regular people. There are open shows sponsored by 4-H or other local horse organizations. There are circuit shows that specialize in a single breed or discipline. There are large state and regional shows that last three to four days. There are prestigious national and international shows that are very important (to somebody). And finally there is the biggest horse show of them all – the Olympics.

Yes, the Olympics is a horse show. It's just like any other horse show. And the reason I know this is because I've seen camera shots of the riders' families sitting in the stands pretending to be awake and acting like they're paying attention. That's exactly what I do! And, as a parent of a horsegirl, you'll be expected to do the same. It's an art, but you'll master it.

Morning of the Horse Show at My House

Surviving a horse show morning brings new meaning to the word "agony." I speak from experience. I've been through it so many times, I think I could do it in my sleep. In fact, that *is* how I do it.

What is a typical horse show morning like? Around our house, it goes like this:

Horse show day begins in the middle of the night. It's dark and it'll be dark for some time. I'm up and moving, but it'll be at least three hours before the onset of noticeable brain wave activity. Everything – people, animals, objects, thoughts – exhibit a surreal quality. I want to throw up.

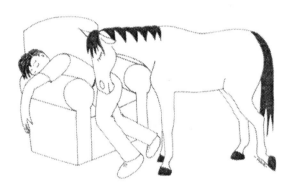

Most of the activity on horse show morning is centered on our family bathroom. The female siblings take up their traditional position inside the bathroom, while the alpha male paces outside the door. From the master bedroom emerges Zombie Wife. "Coffee ... coffee..." she moans. The male grunts and points to the kitchen.

Within the bathroom, the primary activity is bickering. Apparently, one of the females is a sock thief. Denials and counter-accusations fly. There is some non-authorized borrowing of grooming articles. A fresh round of accusations and recriminations result. But nothing is resolved. Somebody is in somebody else's way. And vice versa. The toilet flushes, indicating some progress on that front. The ever-hopeful male crosses his legs.

The bickering is interrupted by a period of relative calm as the females re-generate their verbal energy cells in anticipation of the next round of combat. The muffled sounds of grooming articles being slapped on the sink counter, the clinking and clicking of make-up tools and the squeaking of cupboards opening and shutting indicate continued activity. Peace and progress. Then, out of nowhere an explosion obliterates the quiet:

"FINE! JUST DON'T EVER TOUCH MY HORSE AGAIN!"

The male hobbles out the back door and pees behind a tree.

Hooking Up the Trailer

At some point somebody (me) has to hitch the horse trailer to the truck. Of course, this should be done the previous evening when it's light and no big deal. But at that point, most parents are in a state of denial. Maybe a nuclear war will break out and we won't have to go, is their thinking.

Whether you do it in the dark or light, attaching a horse trailer is governed by four rules. First, The Rule of Too Far. No matter where you stop backing the tow vehicle, the ball will end up either Too Far forward or Too Far back. The second rule, The Rule of Roll, explains the first rule. Even if you managed to get the ball dead center under the hitch, the instant you put the truck in park it will roll either forward or backward just enough so that you can't get it latched without wiggling the trailer post back and forth. This leads to the third rule, The Rule of

Hurt. While wiggling the trailer post back and forth, you will inevitably mash one or more of your fingers. Rule four: bleed.

Packing the Truck and Trailer

Packing the truck and trailer is another job that should be done the night before but never is. There is only one rule in regard to packing for a horse show: The Rule of Forgot It. This rule states that no matter how many things you load into your truck and trailer, there will always be at least one thing you forgot. There is no way around this. Load up the entire contents of your house, storage shed, and barn and you'll still forget something.

Fortunately, everyone is subject to the Rule of Forgot It. The odds that your horse show friends forgot the very same thing you did is slim. So you borrow. And everyone else borrows. The first hour of any horse show is like an open bartering market: "Hey anybody got any hoofblack? I got an extra water bucket!" "We need a lead rope!" "Wife for trade! Zombie Wife for trade!"

Loading the Horses

The most difficult job of the day is loading the horses into the trailer. The reason it's so difficult is not because you're dumb. And it's not because the horse is dumb. It has to do with the past. About 500,000 years of the past. Loading a horse into a horse trailer is a battle against 5,000 centuries of evolution.

The horse has survived the eons by perfecting its best defense against danger: running away. Evolution taught the horse to always have an escape route. Horses feel secure in the open and they instinctively avoid dark enclosed spaces. Dark, enclosed spaces are traditional hiding places for predators. Thus evolution informs the horse that these puny ape-like creatures are trying to squeeze him into a tiny metal box filled with wolves. *Don't go in there, horse,* evolution says.

It's amazing that even one horse in the entire history of horse shows has consented to load. I don't know how other people do it. Maybe it's a matter of training. I suppose if you can convince paratroopers to jump out of perfectly good planes, you can teach a horse to stop fussing and get in there and die like a man. Bad choice of words – but you know what I mean.

How does our family handle the loading problem? Well, we've tried brute force, but this not only proved we were physically weaker than the horse, it also revealed that we weren't much brighter either. I'm not really sure how we do it. We just kind of fight and argue and blame one another until the horse becomes so disgusted with it all, he jumps in the trailer.

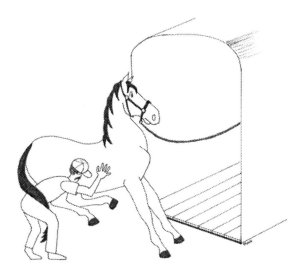

The Trip

Whether the trip to the show grounds is a short jaunt around the block or a journey halfway across the country, you must be aware of one Murphy-like law: *If something can go wrong, it probably already has. You just don't know it yet.*

Here is a partial list of what could go wrong:

...flat tire, brakes lock up, trailer light fail, horse kicks, kid kicks, truck overheats, wife overheats, truck refuses to pull up a hill, radio won't pick up any country stations, radio picks up *only* country stations, missed exit, then missed the next one, last exit six lanes to the left through solid traffic, driver falls asleep, kid throws up, coffee spills, no restroom for next fifty miles, horse colics, electric brakes catch on fire, various windows fly open, clunking sounds from down below, completely forgot to bring: 1) wife, 2) kid, 3) horse.

Parking

Upon arriving at the show grounds, the girls will assault you with a list of parking place demands. The girls want to be near the show ring. The girls want a spot with plenty of shade. The girls want to be by the water. The girls want you to back into this tiny space next to their friends.

The girls are nuts. No person in the entire western hemisphere has the backing skills necessary to do what they ask. But you try anyway. You think everyone else can do it and you don't want to be embarrassed by admitting you can't. So you embarrass yourself even worse by *proving* you can't.

You start by backing up about ten feet. That's the distance it takes to get the truck and trailer hopelessly jackknifed. Then you pull forward twenty feet to straighten it out. You repeat this process until you gradually work yourself a few hundred yards from where you intended to be. At this point, you simply shut off the engine and convince the girls that this – even if it's in the middle of the neighboring cornfield – is the ideal parking lot.

Unloading the Horses

The easiest part of the trip is unloading the horses. They didn't want to be in there in the first place, so open the back door and they will hop right out. Of course, they'll have no idea where they are or how they got there. In fact, from their perspective, they haven't gone anywhere. All they know is that they were squeezed into this deathtrap, they got jostled around a bit, and – SHA-BANG – when the door opens, the whole world around them has been miraculously altered. Horses must wonder how we do that.

Registering

After securing the horses to the trailer, you must register the kids for their classes. Registering is a process in which you write a check for a large sum of money and exchange it for two pieces of paper with tall numbers on them. In addition, all show participants are provided with a "show bill." A show bill is a list of all the show's classes in chronological order. It also includes a few important rules and announcements – the most significant one being, don't bother to ask for your money back.

Local Horse Shows

Local horse shows sponsored by 4-H or other clubs or organizations are often open to all breeds and are usually open to the public. These shows are typically divided into forty to sixty events called *classes*. They are called classes because the kids learn a lot in them.

Some people say that what kids learn most at a horse show is political science. They claim that unlike a real sport where individuals are judged by their ability to knock another human being on his rear end, determining horse show winners is heavily influenced by local horse community politics.

Of course, the idea that politics has anything to do with placings is vehemently and uncategorically denied by the local organizations, the judges, and all first place winners. If you are unsure what a vehement and uncategorical denial is, a good example is when Bill Clinton pointed his finger in the camera and declared, "I did *not* have sexual relations with *that* woman." That was a vehement and uncategorical denial.

At this time, I would like to state my vehement and uncategorical support for local horse show organizations and horse show judges. I personally do not feel that horse show judging has anything to do with politics. I think these people are professionals and they do a wonderful job under difficult circumstances. They are under constant scrutiny and no matter what they decide, somebody is going to be unhappy. I certainly don't want them angry with me, and I want them to like my kids and me, and they all can come over the night before the show and drink my beer and have ice cream. *Good* ice cream. And I always keep a twenty-dollar bill available in case a judge is willing to accept a donation to the Horse Show Judges' Charity Fund.

The Perfect Horse Show

If I had the chance, I'm not sure I would try to improve the current system of judging horse shows. Why create something perfect and mess up all the fun? "Perfect" never happens anyway. And what is and isn't "perfect" depends on who you talk to. For example, according to adolescent horsegirls, a perfect horse show would be a tragic event with Leonardo DiCaprio as the judge. Leo would teach the girls how to spit and almost everyone would die at the end.

Types of Classes:

For Beginners

Beginner's classes include events such as walk-trot and lead-line. Walk-trot is just what it says: participants are only allowed to walk or trot. Cantering and galloping are strictly prohibited, but some participants try it anyway.

In lead-line, wee riders perch on the horse while being led around by a parent or generic big person. A second adult is often present to keep the child from exiting the saddle. Given my level of riding skill, this is the only class I would ever consider entering. I would need two adults to hold me up because I would most certainly be inebriated. One of the adults would have to be Catherine Zeta-Jones.

Standing Classes

The standing classes include events such as showmanship and halter. In these events, the participants lead their horses into the ring and then stand there. And that's it. They don't really do anything. Meanwhile, parents and on-lookers stand outside the ring and watch the participants stand inside the ring. After a while, the judge determines who did the best of job standing there and relays a list of winners to the announcer's stand. Then everybody stands around and waits for the results.

A single standing class can take anywhere from twenty minutes to an hour, depending on the size of the class and the speed of the judge. If the classes are large or if the judge is sadistic, these classes can last all morning and into the afternoon.

Circle Classes

The circle classes include events that require the participants to actually get on their horses and ride them. These include events such as English Equitation (judges the ability of the rider), English Pleasure (judges the horse), English Bareback (an open challenge to the laws of gravity), Western Horsemanship (judges ability of rider to look like a cowboy) and Western Pleasure (judges something, but nobody really knows what).

The circle classes are where the riders get the opportunity to show off their skills and demonstrate their ability to go around and around. In order to keep everybody awake, the judge intermittently asks the riders to change direction or alter the gait. The object here is to get the horse to do what a judge calls for without a great deal of fuss. The class ends when the judge gets sick of the whole thing and orders everybody to line up in the center of the ring.

Jumping Classes

In these classes the horse and rider proceed through a pattern of jumps and turns until the horse wises up and figures out it's easier just to walk around the jumps. Thus, it takes a great deal of training to become a jumper, because you have to totally destroy any logical inclinations the horse may have. Of course, some jumpers are just naturally polite. These horses stop just short of the jump and allow their riders to go over first.

Speed Classes

Also known as "Gymkana" or "Games," these classes include events such as barrel racing, cloverleaf, flag race and relay races. They are normally held toward the end of the show. Since these are timed events, it's easy for even the most horse show-dumb observer to determine who is winning. Riders may be disqualified for various reasons, including lack of forward motion, stepping outside a boundary, running over the timekeeper, and "flipping off" the crowd. But for the most part, it's pretty straightforward competition. Judges seem more relaxed by this part of the show, mainly because by this point, they're just too damn tired to care if anybody bitches at them or not.

Reining and Pattern Classes

In these classes, the riders participate one at a time. The horse and rider proceed through a set pattern and perform natural maneuvers like walking sideways and spinning around on one leg. Not everyone can do these events well. It takes practice. It takes skill. And it takes FOREVER.

Fun Classes

"Fun" classes are typically found toward the end of the show. Until then, participants are prohibited from having fun. But during fun classes, all sorts of zany hell breaks loose. Not really. About the funniest fun class is the one they call Ride-A-Buck. This involves tucking a dollar bill between the saddle and your butt and riding until it falls out. Kids like this event because they think they are supposed to keep the buck when it's over, even though the buck belongs to their parents. However, considering where the dollar has been, adults rarely ask for the buck back.

Trail Class

In trail class, participants see how well their horses react while proceeding through a course containing items typically found in wilderness areas. These items include mailboxes, plastic tarps, automobile tires, abandoned dishwashers, shiny metal objects, and PVC pipes.

Winning

At the conclusion of each class, the judge instructs the participants to line up in the center of the ring. After a short delay and some unspecified messing around, the placings are announced. The winners get to leave first. As they exit the ring dressed in their $1,000 show outfits on their $10,000 horses with their $2,000 saddles, the winners collect their 50-cent ribbons.

Sometimes trophies are awarded to the first place winners. For the remainder of the day, these trophies are proudly displayed upon the hood of the winner's tow vehicle. This leads other less successful participants to conclude that the trophy winner is a "cheater" (*how?*), and a "not recently bathed female of questionable moral character" (or words to that effect), and "an unintelligent member of the canine species" (not male).

Trophies and ribbons are taken home and placed on the dining room table for a day or two and then are put on the winner's bedroom floor. They stay there for approximately three months, and then they are proudly displayed in a cardboard box packed in the attic.

Not Winning

After the placings are announced and the winners leave the ring one by one in glory, the rest of the class is excused *en masse*. Most of the non-winning participants (i.e., L-O-S-E-R-S) take it pretty well. They smile at their friends and family, shrug their shoulders, and think to themselves, *"Gee, I sure would like to KILL something right now..."*

Other riders express themselves vocally. They fume and fuss and carry on about how unfair it is. They blame it on the judge, or the horse, or other riders, or the 4-H leader, or loose dogs, or parents, or a sister, or a brother, or somebody else's sister or brother, or the weather, or the Republican Party. Some say nothing but display their displeasure by throwing some expensive piece of show gear on the ground. This often provokes an angry reprimand from parents, who didn't work hard all week long to pay for that stuff just to have some little brat ruin it in a hissy fit.

Horse Show Experts

While the placings are entirely up to the judge, his or her decisions are subject to review by a group of Horse

Show Experts. These experts can be found at various places outside the ring and they offer their services ABSOLUTELY FREE. While they rarely have any effect upon the judge's decisions, they are never shy about voicing their opinions. They are particularly vocal when a certain rider – usually a family member – is not placed. These experts are known as "mothers."

The Mother-Experts also offer advice to the riders as they go by. Some of their favorite expressions include "Wrong lead! Wrong lead!" (whatever *that* means) and "He's watching you!" (isn't he supposed to be?) and "Ride on the rail, honey! The rail! The rail! Get on the rail!" (physically impossible).

Actually, I'm kind of glad that mothers do this. If they didn't, I would have no way of knowing which riders are having a "good ride" and which ones are just fooling around. To me, they all look pretty much the same. I can pick out the obvious stuff – like when a horse goes by without a rider. Even I know that this is a sign of somebody having a "bad ride." But, other than that, it's a mystery.

Horse Show Mothers

Okay, let's get this straight. Most horse show moms are rational, well-balanced individuals and dedicated parents. The majority of them do not go overboard with horse show competition. They don't look at it as a matter of life and death. They see showing as a way for their child to learn and have fun. It's enough for them that their child participates and enjoys the company of others who share their passion for equestrian events. They are simply there to assist their kid, get through the day with as little trouble as possible, and go home. They are generally laid back about the whole thing and just take it all in perspective and encourage their child to do the same. Nothing seems to bother them and they just kind of float through the day like ho-dee-doe, it's all okay with me.

However, for the mothers who *aren't* heavily sedated or who *don't* drink during the show, the whole thing is pretty much dog-eat-dog. I'm scared of 'em. There are few things in life more terrifying than a horse show mom who sincerely believes her little pumpkin has just been gypped out of a placing. They rip into the judge like they would a box of Godiva raspberry chocolate truffles during *that time* of the month. They yell at other parents or other kids or even the horses. They'll threaten a smart-aleck writer of equine-related, so-called humor that if he even *thinks* of using their outbursts as material for his next piece, he'll soon be joining the Brotherhood of Geldings.

Horse Dads

The noblest of all participants in a horse show are the horse dads. I realize this is difficult for many (about half) of you to accept. But it's true. Fathers play a vital role in the horse show experience. The fact that we're leaning back in lawn chairs with our hands clasped behind our heads and our feet resting on the fender of our trucks while everybody else is scurrying around may appear to the uninformed observer (female) that we're not participating. Nothing could be further from the truth. We are actually engaged in a complex mental procedure that addresses the larger issues of showing horses. For example, what would happen if barbarians from the north attacked the horse show? Would we be ready? What measures would need to be taken? What if a Me-109 fighter plane suddenly appeared and began strafing the announcer's booth? What should we do? Hmm? What happens if there is an earthquake?

I sincerely doubt that even *one* female has given any thought to these issues. It's up to us men. That's because, as most people (about half) know, the male is the Supreme Head and Lord Protector of the family. In our family, for instance, my wife and I have clearly defined lines of authority. I am responsible for making all the big decisions – at a horse show or anywhere else. And she makes all the small ones. Is it my fault that in over twenty years of marriage we have never had a big decision to make?

Of course, fathers do make practical contributions. In fact, it requires certain basic skills to be a horse dad. Chief among these is the ability to spend large sums of money without really knowing why. In addition, he must be able to operate a truck/horse trailer rig (or at least be willing to suffer the humiliation of *trying* to operate one), haul large buckets of water, work the gates, set up jumps, drag the arena, and carry stuff. But only when he is told to.

Sometimes, fathers get cajoled into working special assignments. The most feared assignment is serving as the public address announcer. Since experienced horse dads know that the announcer must be assigned prior to the show, it is often difficult to find an available father at that time. It's because they're hiding. Some find an empty stall in the men's room. Others run out into the woods or seek refuge in neighboring cornfields. A few lurk beneath their trucks.

I've never been asked to serve as the public address announcer. And really, for the psychological well-being of the local horse community and other innocent bystanders, I hope I never am. Because...

This Is How I Would Do It

If I was the public address announcer, here is what everybody would hear at the start of the day:

"... um ... uh ... well ... how do you turn this stupid thing on? Huh? What? It IS on? How did you do that? Where's the button? Oh... I didn't see you do that. When did you do that? I didn't see it... What? They can hear me? No they can't ... They CAN??? Oh brother ..."

A few minutes later:

"Good morning everyone! The disembodied voice you hear is me, THORSE, THE MIGHTY HORSESHOW GOD OF THUNDER! You are my people! Obey me and I will not destroy you!...Anyway, the first class will start in few minutes, so if you have to pee, do it now..."

And then:

"Your attention please! Sponsors for today's show include the 4-H Developmental Committee, Jim's Tack and Feed, Andy's Horseshoein' Service, State Barn Builder's Association and...(yawn)...and...um...(what the heck)...The People's Republic of China and...uh...The U.S. Navy's Adopt a Cruise Missile Program, The William Jefferson Clinton School for Girls, The Central Intelligence Agency and...uh... K-Mart."

During a class, the announcer receives his instructions from the judge, who stands in the middle of the show ring. This is accomplished by a complex system of communication whereby the judge whispers to an assistant what he wants the horses to do next. The assistant uses a powerful walkie-talkie thingie to relay these instructions to the announcer's stand. By this process, bewildered police officers throughout the local area receive orders like "Trot your horses, trot please" and "Bring 'em in and line 'em up facing the judge."

Since the announcer is bound by tradition to repeat word for word what the judge wants, this leaves him with very little to say about what goes on in the ring. Left out of the decision making process, the announcer is denied the opportunity to express his creative impulses and is unable to explore the rich possibilities of individual expression. It's a damn shame.

If I were the announcer, I'd challenge this tradition. For example, if the judge indicated he wanted to see a trot, here is what I'd do:

"The judge wants you to trot your horses again...Don't do it! Canter your horses instead! Yeah, canter, pleas...No, on second thought, turn your horse around and walk. But only half of you. If your last name has less than seven letters, turn around and canter. The rest of you can continue at a walk...nah, go ahead and trot...No, canter! No, trot! No, walk! Okay, if you are cantering now, I want you to walk and if you're walking now switch to a canter and if you are trotting, I want you to spit on the judge when you go by him. Spit, please..."

At this point, it's entirely possible that an angry mob of parents, riders, 4-H officials, dogs, and one slightly moistened judge would be clamoring its way to the announcer's stand. As they hauled me away, I would inform them that I would be available next week if they needed a show chairman.

Big Shows

Most local shows last a single day. However, there are shows that run several days and even a few that continue over the course of two to three weeks. This is not just an idle threat; it's the God-honest truth. They have them like that.

I have been to some three-day shows. It's just like a one-day show except that instead of waiting two to three hours between three-minute riding classes, you drive five hours to wait six hours between three-minute riding classes.

Most county and state fairs have an equine element. These are essentially shows that are spread out over several days, with camping available. Bathroom facilities vary from place to place but most are supported by state and county funds and we all know how government officials feel about this sort of thing.

Show Clothes

The first thing you need to understand about show clothes is that each style of riding has its own outfit. Thus, what your little pumpkinseed wears for hunt seat will not do for saddle seat, and saddle seat clothes have nothing to do with western events and so on. And on. And on. And on.

English riding clothes feature an item called breeches. Breeches is the term for a type of short trousers that cover the hips and thighs and fit snugly just below the knee. Sometimes people who are new to riding don't know what breeches are for. "I don't need those," they think. "My regular jeans are good enough," they believe. These people will discover the meaning of another term later on in the day. "Severe chafing" is what they learn. And they won't need to look it up in the dictionary.

Sometimes a rider needs clips or straps to keep the "jods" from "riding up." What is a "jod," you ask? Well, I dunno. But apparently, if they ride up, it's no good. You may find yourself shouting, "Oh, my jod!" Sorry.

Your child will also need some kind of jacket (one for each style of riding), boots (two for each style of riding), spurs, helmets, cowboy hats, western shirts, chaps, and gloves. And don't forget the bracelet and a key fob! A fob is critical for her success.

She'll need a stock tie or a Velcro® collar and perhaps a bib-front stock tie. A gold-plated stock pin would be nice. They come in a variety of shapes including snaffle bits, hunting horns, horseheads, and satanic symbols.

Other wardrobe considerations include an equestrian hairnet or French barrette net, sport bra tanks and, of course, padded riding underwear with knit terry crotch. And by all means, don't forget the minimal-bounce bra (one for each style of riding)!

The End of Horse Show Day

It won't seem like it while you're there, but all horse shows end sooner or later. Usually later. For most parents, this is a time of great rejoicing and hasty packing. Just throw everything – including the stuff you borrowed – into the back of the truck. Then inform the child, "You can sort it all out tomorrow." Anything that's not yours can be lent to someone at the next show.

Our family concludes horse show day with the traditional meal of beer, pizza, and beer. This is consumed while watching a video of whatever the person with the most energy left decides to put on. By now, everybody is too exhausted to be picky. And now, as we roost motionless in front of some mind-numbing video, the entire family is finally in sync.

CHAPTER 12:

An Open Letter to the Equine Species

Dear Horses:

I know I've complained a lot about the way you burst in and took over our lives. The time and money we spent on you would have gone a long way toward a nicer house, newer cars, or better therapists. But I want you to know something: it hasn't been all that bad. I don't want you horses thinking I don't like you. Believe me, I *do* like you.

I'm going to be honest. I like dogs more than horses. Please don't take this personally. I'm not saying dogs are better than you, just different. I can look my dog in the eye – both eyes – and we understand each other. You allow eye contact, but it's more out of curiosity than anything else. I can overcome your casual indifference with an apple or by stroking your neck in that special spot, but there will always be something that separates us. I can share a hamburger with my dog.

Just because I'm not horse crazy doesn't mean you haven't added something to my life. I've discovered that hanging around the places where your species and mine come together – the barn, the pasture, the fence line - lifts my spirits. There is something about your company that makes me feel a little saner.

I want to tell you about what you have done for the people closest to me. My wife, Jenny, has always been an animal lover. But for most of her life, she preferred to appreciate you from a distance. A childhood history of bites and kicks led her to avoid close contact with horses. I'm sure this was all a result of a misunderstanding, but trust *is* a two-way street.

An amazing thing happened after you came into our lives: Jenny got to know and trust you again. While she retained a healthy respect for your size and unpredictability, her confidence grew until she thought nothing of standing in the midst of thirty horses assisting her daughters as they waited to enter the next class.

You helped us guide Jamie and Hiliary into adulthood. In the process, you became a part of them. Hiliary is a nurturer with a well-developed affinity for kids and the elderly. Jamie is poised and self-confident, the kind of person who pours herself into everything she does. Both girls began displaying these traits around the time you arrived.

It's possible that Jamie and Hiliary would have grown up just fine without you. Who really knows? What I do know is that taking care of you – a creature with so many needs – taught them about responsibility. Learning to handle you gave them confidence. These things are not easily taught nor do they come naturally to humans. Unlike you, we don't walk on our first day.

Because of you, we spent more time together as a family. It seemed like we were always preparing for a horse show, at a horse show, or recovering from one. Weekends we would have otherwise spent going in different directions became our family time. We had our share of arguments, but we also had a lot of fun.

But what about you? You seem to tolerate the shows and I think you enjoy being among your own kind. Like us, you are social creatures. But I don't believe the competition has any meaning to you. My guess is that you would prefer a nice walk in the woods or a quiet afternoon grazing in the pasture.

I've often wondered how you feel about living with humans. If given the chance, would you choose to be free of us? Let's face it, you did not ask to be with people. We chose you. Humans were given dominion over the world's creatures and you are one of the animals we picked to live with us. At first, we did this because you were useful. But now, we keep you because we like you. In the last 10,000 years we have developed a strong affection for your species. You are a part of our history, our culture, and our dreams. You've been with us too long and you've become too much a part of us to let go.

What you give us is invaluable. But what about our obligation to you? When we domesticated you, we separated you from your natural environment – the environment for which evolution shaped you. Beneath the thin coating of domestication, you retain the primal physical and psychological needs of the natural horse. As your keepers, it is our obligation to understand these needs and to compensate for what you no longer receive from nature. When we do this well, you live a pretty good life with us. When we are unaware of your needs or do a poor job meeting them, you become miserable and sick and neurotic.

Fortunately for you, there are people among my species who have no greater desire than to see to your happiness. In fact, the rest of us have a hard time holding them back. Those of us who stand at the periphery of your world often worry that our horse-crazed loved ones are obsessed. We tell them there is more to life than horses and that it would be healthy for them to develop other interests.

This is wrong. Instead of trying to hold them back, we should allow them to revel in their passion. An addiction overwhelms an individual's personality and distorts his or her identity. A genuine passion allows them to discover who they really are. This kind of self-awareness should not only be encouraged, it should be celebrated.

While we should encourage the horse lover's passion, we should also help them focus it. Undirected, passion has a tendency to dissipate or even degenerate into something harmful. Without direction there is no purpose and it is easy to lose sight of what is really important. When small desires like blue ribbons or social status take precedence over your physical and psychological needs, we not only fail to meet our obligation to you, but we also betray what is best in us. And it becomes easy for everyone involved to slip into cynicism and indifference. That's when you suffer.

The passion of horsepeople is the only thing that gives humans the right to claim kinship with your sensitive species. While the affection for you runs deep in the human psyche, it is strongest and most effectual with them. Without it, your condition is reduced to that of any other large livestock. It is a passion easily recognized in the horse crazy kid, but it also endures in the most mature and accomplished horseperson. This passion is what motivates the former to learn and the latter to teach. And if you are to have the best possible life with us, then my species must forever learn and teach.

Thanks for being around. Without you, the world would be a less sane place.

Sincerely yours,

Bob Goddard

Affiliated Publications

Looking for articles by Bob Goddard? Check out one of these great horse publications.

The Trail Rider America's premier trail and pleasure riding magazine. Published bi-monthly, circulated nationally. Rene Riley Editor, 730 Front Street, Louisville, CO 80027 www.trailridermagazine.com

Phelps Equestrian Sports Network PhelpsSports.com is a new and highly innovative equestrian sports website offering equestrians and fans of equestrian sports from around the world a single web address for the latest breaking news from the high performance disciplines. 13833 Wellington Trace, Unit E-4 #221 Wellington, Florida 33414. www.phelpssports.com

Flying Changes A monthly northwest sporthorse magazine. 19502 NE 134th Place, Battle Ground, WA 98604. Lauren Baker, editor/publisher. www.flyingchanges.com

Horses All Canada's leading equine newspaper. Publishing horse news and information since 1977. 49 White Oak Crescent SW, Calgary, Alberta, Canada T3C 3J9. www.horsesall.com

Apples & Oats All breed, all discipline magazine devoted to horse lovers in Iowa and throughout the Midwest. Carol Eilers, Editor. 5070 Northridge Point SE, Cedar Rapids, IA 52403. www.applesnoats.com

Saddle Up! Magazine A monthly publication devoted to Michigan and Ohio horse lovers. 8415 Hogan Road,

Fenton, Michigan 48430. www.saddleupmag.com (810) 714-9000.

Northwest Rider Magazine Regional monthly all-breed magazine based in Oregon. Valrey Van Gundy, Editor. P.O. Box 607 Newberg, OR 97132. www.nwrider.com

Horse & Pony News An all breed, all discipline paper published every first and third Friday of the month. Sally Alford, Editor. P.O. Box 2050, Seffner, FL 33583. www.adairmag.com/links/link_horsepony.html

The Pony Press All Breed/All Discipline Equine Newspaper. Published bi-monthly and distributed free throughout Missouri and surrounding area. Cheryl Childs, Managing Editor. ESP Publications, P.O. Box 1968, Ozark, MO 65721. www.theponypress.com

Northern Horse Source An all breed, all discipline high quality equine magazine based in North Pole, Alaska. Published bi-monthly. Sandy Davis, Editor. P.O. Box 56539 , North Pole, AK 99705. www.northernhorsesource.com (907) 488-8088

California Riding Magazine Regional all-breed all-discipline magazine. 9131 Chesapeake Dr., San Diego, CA 92123. www.ridingmagazine.com

Mid-Atlantic Horse A large regional all-breed all-discipline publication serving the New York – Virginia region. David Yeats-Thomas, Editor. P.O. Box 609, Ephrata PA 17522. www.mid-atlantichorse.com

GREEN GRASS SYNDICATED FEATURES, Marcia King, Owner. Features hard copy catalog offering more than

300 articles on a variety of equine subjects at modest prices. Includes previously published material from top equine writers and journalists. 2972 115th St. Toledo, OH 43611-2838

www.geocities.com/greengrasssyndicated
GreenGrassSyndicated@yahoo.com

The Author and the Illustrator

Bob Goddard

As an equine humorist, Bob has written over eighty articles for thirty different national and regional horse publications. He lives in Ravenna, Michigan with wife Jenny and their naughty, but gradually improving dog, Jessie. Visit Bob at www.horsecrazy.net.

Laurie Mackenzie

Illustrator Laurie Mackenzie draws and paints in upstate New York. She has created illustrations for several books, including two for her husband, Steve. Surrounded by glorious countryside, family and a small pack of dogs, she feels life is best viewed from the back of a horse or through the camera's lens.

Printed in the United States
200079BV00004B/1-156/A

9 781601 452580